Alfred's Teach Yourself Mixing

DAVID TERRY

Everything you need to know to start mixing now!

- **Step-by-step approach for successfully mixing music**

- **Covers EQ**, panning, compressors, expanders, reverb, delay, vocal tuning, and other effects

- **Techniques for creating both digital audio and analog mixes**

Alfred Music Publishing Co., Inc.
P.O. Box 10003
Van Nuys, CA 91410-0003
alfred.com

ISBN-10: 0-7390-6987-X
ISBN-13: 978-0-7390-6987-5

Cover photo of the TASCAM DM-4800 courtesy of TASCAM

Contents printed on environmentally responsible paper.

CONTENTS

CHAPTER 1. IF IT SOUNDS GOOD, IT IS GOOD . . . 3

CHAPTER 2. YOUR LISTENING ENVIRONMENT . . . 4
Acoustic Treatments 4
Monitoring 5
Mixing Platform 6
Getting Used to Your Room 6

CHAPTER 3. EQUALIZATION 7
What Is an EQ, and
  Why Would You Use One? 7
Frequency and Pitch 8
Types of EQs and Their Controls 9
  Peak Filters 9
  Shelving EQs 11
  High- and Lowpass Filters 12
EQ and Ear Training 13
EQs In Use 14
Choosing an EQ 15
Subtractive Vs. Additive EQ 16
EQing the Low End 16
EQing the Low Mids 19
EQing the Mids and High Mids 20
EQing the High End 21
● Quick Guide: Instrument Frequency Ranges 21

CHAPTER 4. DYNAMICS PROCESSORS 22
Compressors 22
  What Are Compressors, and
  Why Would You Use One? 22
  Types of Compressors 22
  The Controls 23
  Compression vs. Limiting 24
  Multiband Compressors 25
  Sidechaining 26
  Parallel Compression 27
  Compressors as Tone Devices 30
  Is Louder Better? 31
  Compressors In Use 32
  Choosing a Compressor 34
  The Sound of Compression 34
  ● *QuikGuide:Converting Milliseconds to Beats per Minute* . . . 35
  Compressing Instruments with a
  Wide Dynamic Range 36
  Compression Instruments with a
  Small Dynamic Range 39
  Compressing Bass 40
  Compressing Vocals 41
  De-essing 44
  Bus Compression 48
  Other Creative Compression 50
Expanders 54
  What Are Expanders, and
  Why Would You Use One? 54
  The Controls 55
  Expanders In Use 55

Noise Gates 56
  What Are Noise Gates, and
  Why Would You Use One? 56
  The Controls 57
  Noise Gates In Use 57

CHAPTER 5. SPACE: REVERBS, DELAYS ETC. 58
Reverb 58
  What Is Reverb, and Why Do I Need It? 58
  The Controls 59
  Types of Reverbs 60
  Reverbs In Use 60
  Choosing a Reverb 62
  Incorporating EQ and Other Processing 63
  Which Instruments Should Have
  Reverb On Them? 65
Delay 65
  What Is Delay, and
  Why Do I Need It? 65
  Types Of Delay Processors 65
  The Controls 66
  ● *QuikGuide: Note-to-BPM Conversion* 66
  Delay In Use 67

CHAPTER 6. OTHER EFFECTS 71
  Modulation Effects 71
  Distortion 72
  Stereo Image Enhancement 73

CHAPTER 7. BEFORE YOU START YOUR MIX . . . 74
Editing 74
Vocal Tuning 74
Sound Replacement 76
Some Thoughts On Panning 78

CHAPTER 8. KEEPING IT MANAGEABLE! 81
Getting Organized 81
Setting Up the Mixer 82
Groups, Buses and FX Returns 83
Additional Mix Preparations 85

CHAPTER 9. THE MIX! 87
Deciding On an Approach 87
North and South 89
Low Frequencies 90
Mid- and High-Range Frequencies 91
Build the Foundation First 91
Start With the Star 92
All In 92
Automation 92
To Sum the Mix 95

INDEX 96

IF IT SOUNDS GOOD, IT IS GOOD

"If it sounds good, it is good." That, in a nutshell, is the idea at the core of mixing. It sounds easy, right? Well, it's not! Mixing is one of the most difficult processes in audio engineering. Mixing is neither all technical nor all artistry; rather, it is a well-balanced blend of the two. As a mix engineer, you'll need to be able to capture the artistry through the technical. This is a difficult task that usually takes years to master. There are many forces fighting against achieving a great mix: too much dynamic content, not enough dynamic content, too many instruments occupying the same frequency space, too many instruments occupying the same place in the stereo field, a sound that's too muddy, a sound that's too bright, not getting enough sleep, or not enough impact—just to name a few. It is the job of the mix engineer to take the multitrack recordings and create a mix that conveys the emotion and impact of the song. As mix engineers, we need to create impact and excitement through the creative use of tools like EQ, compression, reverbs, delays and automation. In other words, we need to make it sound good, so it is good!

This book is by no means intended to be a mixing bible that should be quoted chapter and verse to all of your friends. However, by reading, understanding and applying the techniques I describe, you should be able to get enough basics down to impress friends, family and other musicians with your mixing skills. And, who knows? If you keep applying your knowledge, you might just be able to create something that will take you to the top of the charts! Let's get started…

CHAPTER 2 YOUR LISTENING ENVIRONMENT

Ultimately, your listening environment is the space between your ears—and if that is broken, all of the books in the world won't help you. I'm going to assume that the part between your ears is fine, and focus and the part that can be changed. So before you fire up your mixer, it is important to make sure that what you are hearing in your studio is an accurate reproduction of the music you are mixing. Whether your control room is a bedroom, garage, bonus room, vacant house, or a commercial facility, the physics of sound reproduction in the room needs to be addressed. Since this book is about the mixing process and not about studio design, and because I am not an expert on studio construction, I am not going to go into great detail about the science involved in acoustically treating your studio. It is, however, a very important part of the process, because a poorly designed mixing environment will lead to mixes that only your hearing impaired dog will enjoy. There are, however, some cost-effective solutions for improving the acoustics in project or home studios.

Acoustic Treatments

Soundwaves travel through the air and bounce off some surfaces, and are absorbed by others. Different frequencies sometimes behave in different ways: Higher frequencies can easily reflect, or bounce off of hard surfaces, while lower frequencies can build up in corners of a room and travel easily through walls into another room. In addition to keeping the neighbors' complaints to a minimum, the main goals of acoustic treatments are to prevent rogue soundwaves from affecting the frequency response, eliminate echoes or flutter, keep sound from leaking out of (or into) the studio, and to improve the low-end accuracy of the room.

The two main types of treatments used to accomplish these goals are diffusers and absorbers. Diffusers are used to reduce or eliminate reflections (echoes) arising from parallel surfaces (like the four walls, ceiling and floor) in your control room. Absorbers control echoes and can reduce the overall reverb time (basically, length of echoes; we'll go into this later) of the room as well as alter the frequency response.

▲ *Examples of different studio environments. Top, a tracking room; bottom, a control room. (The Tracking Room, Nashville)*

If you are using one of the very common bedroom or basement setups, it is not likely that you can talk your parents or significant other into paying to have your house redesigned to accommodate your mixing room. You can, however, buy treatment kits that are designed to dramatically improve the listening environment of small home studios. Some makers of acoustic materials, such as Auralex (www.auralex.com), even have an online configuration tool to help you determine what you need based on the room dimensions you supply. Take a break from the online games and search the Internet, and you'll find lots of useful information on this subject. You may not build a million-dollar control room on your own, but you can make a big difference without having to steal your sister's piggy bank to pay for it!

▲ *Acoustic foam*

Monitoring

This term does not refer to your computer screen or the "monitor" you may have fastened around your ankle. I'm talking about the speakers in your studio. The speakers you choose play a very important role in the outcome of your mix. Basing your decision on how many windows the speakers can break within a 100-yard radius is probably not the smartest approach to take; flat (even at different frequencies) and accurate should be at the top of the wish list. Just like improving room acoustics, choosing accurate speakers ensures your mixes will sound the same everywhere—i.e. they'll rock just as hard in a 1968 Super Beetle as they do in your studio.

Every mix engineer has his or her favorite set of speakers to mix on. Some engineers like to mix on total garbage speakers—the idea being that if the mix sounds great on your horrible, ten-dollar computer speakers, it will sound good on Aunt Elma's clock radio. Other mix engineers prefer totally flat, even, pristine speakers. It really boils down to what you have become accustomed to; I recommend using both. Having both flat, good sounding-speakers and a set of computer speakers will give you the tools to please your hip-hop loving cousin and good old Aunt Elma.

After you have decided on which speakers you want, you need to place them in an optimal position. Your room dimensions and acoustics are determining factors, but generally, you want to keep speakers away from the walls and at ear level.

Mixing Platform

There are endless debates about the sonic superiority of analog mixing vs. digital mixing, vs. pie-in-the-sky mixing, vs. every other way you can think of mixing. Regardless of the equipment you have at your disposal, I believe the greatest piece of gear in any studio is the one sitting at the controls! As you read through this book, you'll notice that I use DAWs (digital audio workstations) as my frame of reference for most of the examples. But most of the principles and practices here apply, whether you use analog or digital mixing. So don't get too focused on the tools in front of you. Are they important? Absolutely! But you can achieve a great mix with virtually any equipment, once you understand the principles.

Getting Used to Your Room

Spend some time getting used to the "sound" of your room. By this, I mean listening, listening and more listening. Listen to a few familiar CDs in another studio, on your home stereo and in your car. Take note of what you hear in the low, mid, and high frequencies. Then take those same CDs into your studio and listen. Write down the differences you hear. If everything sounds better in your car, then you might consider some sort of a wireless mixing setup so you can mix while in the drive-thru at McDonalds...or, you could try to park your car in your control room...hmmm, maybe you should just read on.

EQUALIZATION

CHAPTER 3

What Is an EQ, and Why Would You Use One?

There used to be a TV show in the '80s about a gun-toting vigilante called The Equalizer, but that is not at all what I'm referring to. An EQ or equalizer is a filter or set of filters that allow you to alter the frequency content of an audio signal in some way. (We'll talk about time- and level-based processing in the next chapters.) Like oil filters remove unwanted dirt particles from your car's engine, these EQs are used for removing unwanted noise, compensating for unbalanced frequencies, improving fidelity, or emphasizing a frequency area. (You've probably played around with a graphic EQ on a home stereo.) EQs can dramatically color the sound, or be very transparent. They can even be used as a creative tool to make your amazing acoustic guitar sound like it was recorded underwater through a telephone.

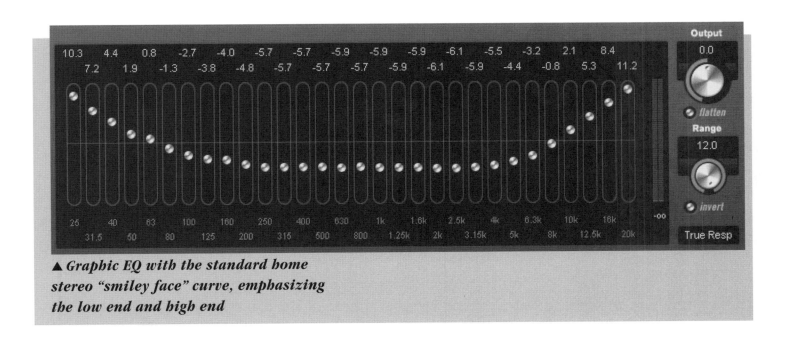

▲ *Graphic EQ with the standard home stereo "smiley face" curve, emphasizing the low end and high end*

Frequency and Pitch

When starting a mix, it is good to understand the relationship between audio frequency and musical pitch. All sounds that you hear are made up of tones generated by pressure waves of air molecules. The differences we hear in pitch are caused by the rate of the soundwaves as they travel to our ears. Lower-pitched sounds travel in longer wave cycles that are spaced farther apart, and higher-pitched sounds travel in shorter wave cycles that are spaced closer together. The number of times a soundwave cycles per second, a.k.a its frequency, is measured in Hertz (Hz). Musicians call the pitch in the center of a keyboard Middle C, while scientists (and engineers) call the same note 261.626 Hz. That just means that the waveform for Middle C cycles 261.626 times per second. Why is this important? Other than the fact that you just got a little smarter, when mixing a song there might be some unwanted frequencies building up when you add multiple instruments all playing the same note or chord. Unwanted build-up can be easily addressed if you know the musical key of the song and translate those notes into frequencies, then EQ them.

Octave	Pitch	Hertz	Octave	Pitch	Hertz	Octave	Pitch	Hertz	Octave	Pitch	Hertz	Octave	Pitch	Hertz
0	C	16	1	C	33	2	C	65	3	C	131			
0	C#	17	1	C#	35	2	C#	69	3	C#	139			
0	D	18	1	D	37	2	D	73	3	D	147			
0	D#	20	1	D#	39	2	D#	78	3	D#	156			
0	E	21	1	E	41	2	E	82	3	E	165			
0	F	22	1	F	44	2	F	87	3	F	175	Octave	Pitch	Hertz
0	F#	23	1	F#	46	2	F#	93	3	F#	185	8	C	4186
0	G	25	1	G	49	2	G	98	3	G	196	8	C#	4435
0	G#	26	1	G#	52	2	G#	104	3	G#	208	8	D	4699
0	A	28	1	A	55	2	A	110	3	A	220	8	D#	4978
0	A#	29	1	A#	58	2	A#	117	3	A#	233	8	E	5274
0	B	31	1	B	62	2	B	124	3	B	247	8	F	5588
												8	F#	5920
4	C	262	5	C	523	6	C	1047	7	C	2093	8	G	6272
4	C#	278	5	C#	554	6	C#	1109	7	C#	2218	8	G#	6645
4	D	294	5	D	587	6	D	1175	7	D	2349	8	A	7040
4	D#	311	5	D#	622	6	D#	1245	7	D#	2489	8	A#	7459
4	E	330	5	E	659	6	E	1319	7	E	2637	8	B	7902
4	F	349	5	F	699	6	F	1397	7	F	2794			
4	F#	370	5	F#	740	6	F#	1475	7	F#	2960			
4	G	392	5	G	784	6	G	1568	7	G	3136			
4	G#	415	5	G#	831	6	G#	1661	7	G#	3322			
4	A	440	5	A	880	6	A	1760	7	A	3520			
4	A#	466	5	A#	932	6	A#	1885	7	A#	3729			
4	B	494	5	B	988	6	B	1976	7	B	3951			

▲ *Musical-notes-to-frequency conversion chart*

Types of EQs and Their Controls

Equalization filters come in three types: peak, shelving and pass filters (high- and lowpass). EQs can use passive or active electronic elements, digital algorithms, or even vacuum tubes to shape the tone of the source audio signal. (Contrary to what you might think, vacuum tubes used for audio purposes do not create a sucking sound like a vacuum cleaner.) Digital EQs use programming algorithms instead of electronic elements to alter the signal. Both analog and digital EQs generally use the same set of controls to alter the frequency content.

Peak Filters

Peak filters are the most flexible and probably the most often-used filter types. They have three variables or controls: frequency, Q and cut/boost.

The frequency control, as the name suggests, allows you to select the center frequency of the peak filter. Peak filters operate using a bell curve, in which equalization is heaviest at a center frequency that falls at the top, or peak, of the bell curve. This process allows for smooth operation across a wide range of frequencies.

The Q control adjusts the width of the bell curve. By changing the Q, you can adjust the width of the frequency range around the chosen center frequency. A higher Q setting will affect a narrow bandwidth around the center frequency. A lower Q setting will affect a wider bandwidth around the center frequency. See examples on page 10.

The cut/boost or gain control determines the level of the selected frequencies. A cut, or gain reduction, will make the frequencies softer; a boost, or gain increase, will make the frequency selection louder.

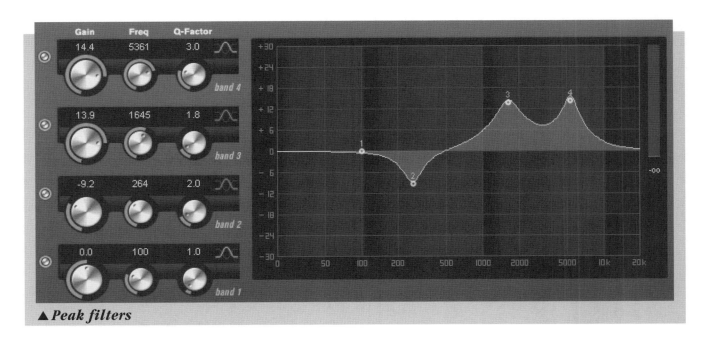

▲ *Peak filters*

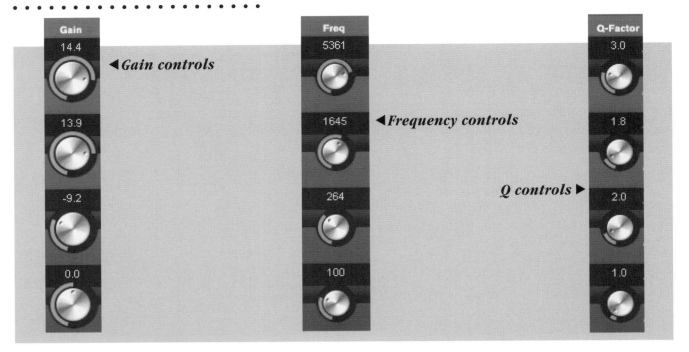

◄ *Gain controls*

◄ *Frequency controls*

Q controls ▶

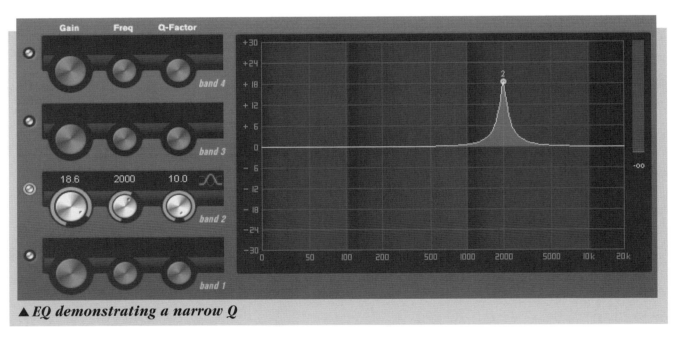

▲ *EQ demonstrating a narrow Q*

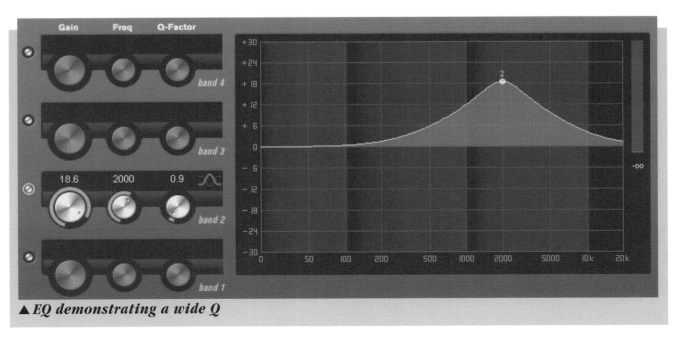

▲ *EQ demonstrating a wide Q*

Shelving EQs

Shelving EQs either boost or cut everything above or below a selected cutoff frequency by an equal amount. There are two types of shelving EQs: high-shelf and low-shelf. The most common types of shelving filters are the bass and treble controls found in a car or home stereo system. The frequency control determines the cutoff frequency of the filter: If a high-shelf filter is being used and the frequency control is set to 2 kHz, all the frequencies above 2 kHz will be affected. Likewise, if a low-shelf is being used and the frequency control is set to 300 Hz, all the frequencies below 300 Hz will be affected. The cut/boost, or gain, control either adds or subtracts the selected frequency range to or from the audio material. All shelving filters have a cut/boost and frequency control; some also have an adjustable slope control, which determines how steep the filter will roll off from the selected frequency after gain has been adjusted. Higher slope values will result in a steeper frequency roll-off, and lower values will result in a flatter, more gentle roll-off from the selected frequency.

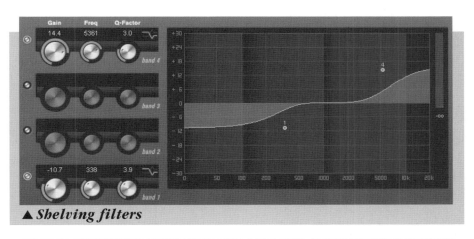

▲ *Shelving filters*

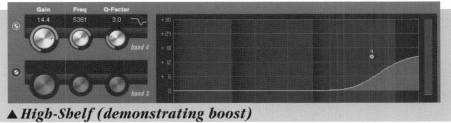

▲ *High-Shelf (demonstrating boost)*

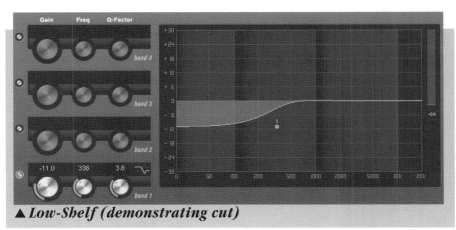

▲ *Low-Shelf (demonstrating cut)*

High- and Lowpass Filters

High- and lowpass filters function as their names suggest: A highpass filter allows high frequencies to pass through while filtering out low frequencies; lowpass filters allow low frequencies to pass through while filtering out high frequencies. All high and lowpass filters have a selectable frequency control, and some have a slope adjustment.

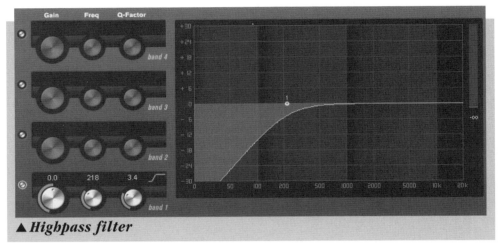

▲ *Highpass filter*

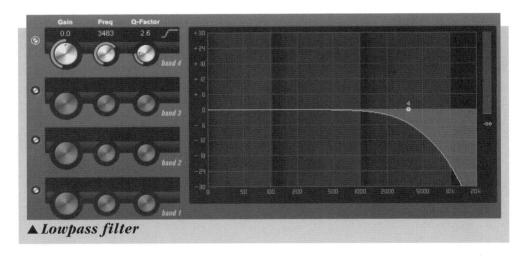

▲ *Lowpass filter*

The frequency control determines the frequency where audio signal will be altered: When using a highpass filter with the frequency control set to 100 Hz, all of the frequencies below 100 Hz will be filtered out, allowing all of the frequencies above 100 Hz to pass through. Likewise, a lowpass filter with the frequency control set to 5 kHz will filter out everything above 5 kHz, allowing the lower frequencies to pass through.

The pass filter's slope control sets how steeply, in dB per octave, the frequencies are attenuated. In practice, this is similar to the Q adjustment on other filters; setting a higher number of dB per octave will result in a steeper curve, while a lower number will have a gentler curve.

EQ and Ear Training

The more you mix, the easier it will become to identify different frequencies. It's a great idea to do some ear-training exercises from time to time so you can enter the strongest ears contest in your city and, more importantly, quickly dial in EQ changes.

One way to create your own ear-training exercise is to insert a pink noise generator on a signal path in your studio. Then insert a 1/3-octave graphic EQ after the pink noise generator. (A graphic EQ is a set of peak filters that uses a series of sliders, faders or rotary knobs to cut the boost of certain frequencies. The Q factor on each frequency band is fixed. The term 1/3-octave refers to the number of EQ filters per octave. So a 1/3-octave EQ has three EQ filters per octave, with each filter band centered 1/3-octave away from the adjacent filter.)

Start by performing a significant boost on each of the 31 bands, one after another, so you can easily determine how the sound is being altered. Repeat this process three or four times, using as much of a gain boost on each of the bands as possible.

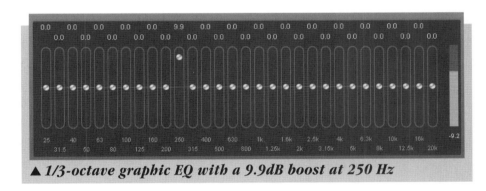

▲ *1/3-octave graphic EQ with a 9.9dB boost at 250 Hz*

Now, repeat the test. But this time, only boost each band half as much as you did before. If you started off with a boost of 12 dB, add a 6dB boost this time. You should still notice the change, especially as you become more familiar with the sound you create when you boost each of the EQ bands.

Next, try cutting each band instead of boosting. This will be more difficult to discern than the boosts. Start with a substantial cut so you can easily hear the difference. Repeat this test until you feel comfortable recognizing each frequency band. Repeat this test cutting each band by half the level you cut before.

Now, try performing the same test with some familiar audio program material. Play a few CDs that you like and boost and cut the 31 bands on the graphic EQ. Note which instruments are affected by each of the different bands. This will give you a good idea of the frequency ranges where the instruments "speak." (There are a number of tests like this available online.)

EQS In Use

In addition to removing unwanted frequencies from specific instruments or stereo mixes, EQs can affect the perceived "distance" of elements in the mix from the listener. "Bright" instruments, or instruments with more high-frequency information are perceived as being closer and more up-front in the mix, while "darker" ones appear more distant. By using a high-shelving EQ to cut high frequencies, you can effectively push things farther back in your mix. Likewise, boosting the upper mids and/or high frequencies will bring things more up-front and in-your-face.

Getting used to instruments and voices competing for the same frequency space in your mix can be a tough job. A common mistake used in an attempt to give the impression of more space is to pan mix elements (move them left and right) in the stereo field. While this technique is definitely an important part of the mixing process, it is not a substitute for properly EQing your tracks. This is why I highly recommend making initial EQ adjustments while listening in mono. That's right, mono! No, this isn't 1956, but mixing in mono can do wonders for your ability to discern where instruments in your mix are fighting over the same frequency range. This is because you aren't fooled into thinking you have adequate frequency space in your mix due to left/right placement across a stereo field; switching to mono centers everything so you can really hear which instruments are masking other ones.

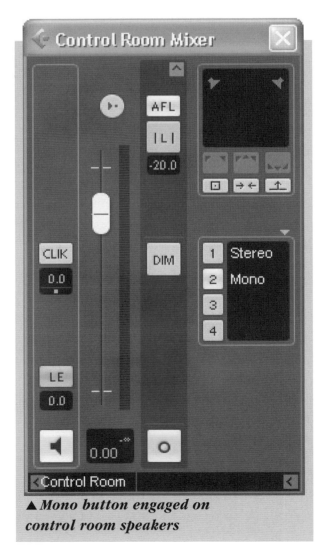

▲ *Mono button engaged on control room speakers*

Choosing an EQ

There are many factors to consider when choosing an EQ for mixing. What does the source signal need? Does it need some "air" added in the upper frequencies? Does it need some low/mid frequencies removed? Does it just need a notch with a high Q to get rid of a problem area? Do you need to hire someone else to mix your project? Regardless of the EQ question, there is most likely an EQ that has the answer. There are a wide variety of unique equipment designs, and they all have different strengths. For example, a certain high-shelving filter may sound particularly good on a vocal but might not sound as good on drum overheads, because some filter designs may accentuate unwanted frequencies in the cymbals, but those same designs may add just the right amount of air to a particular vocal.

Highpass filters with fixed slopes aren't always the best choice for rolling out rumble on certain instruments. If the slope is too steep, you may end up making them too thin. Likewise, if the slope is too gradual, it may not take out enough rumble or room noise.

It's important to familiarize yourself with all of your EQ tools. Some EQs will impart their own sound just by being added to the signal path; others will be very transparent. Use trial and error to learn different characteristics and decide what works best for a given application. Spend some time using different EQs on different sources; hear what sounds good and what doesn't. Keep in mind that a certain EQ for a particular source on one mix won't necessarily be the best choice for that same source on another mix. You need to practice what all our parents told us we never did when we were teenagers: listen, listen, listen, and listen some more.

Subtractive Vs. Additive EQ

Should you boost the high end or cut the low end? Ultimately, taking either approach can net a similar result, and you should do whichever sounds best for the song. However, I think that the better place to start is by using subtractive EQ. Cutting instead of boosting gives a more natural sound across the frequency spectrum, in my opinion. While this isn't always the case, I think it is a safer place to start. Remember to experiment with both approaches and hear the difference for yourself. If it sounds good, it is good!

EQing the Low End

Does your mix need a big, fat bottom? If it does, you'll find the low end or bass frequencies in the 16 to 250Hz range, and sub-bass frequencies in the 20 to 80Hz range. The sub-bass frequencies are usually felt more than they are heard, and can add a sense of power in the mix. But be very careful not to add too many sub-bass frequencies; you may end up needing Weight Watchers for audio mixes when that big bottom end chews through a few speakers!

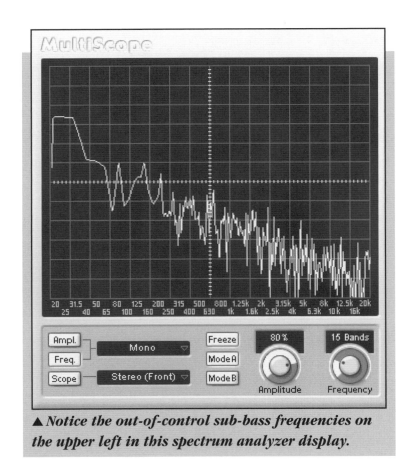

▲ *Notice the out-of-control sub-bass frequencies on the upper left in this spectrum analyzer display.*

In a typical pop or rock production, elements that often reside in the sub-bass frequency band include kick drum, bass guitar, certain loops, synth pads, organs, pianos, and a few orchestral instruments like double bass and cello. That doesn't necessarily mean all of the elements need to be occupying that space in the mix at the same time; you'll need to make that decision on a case-by-case basis. There are also sub-bass frequencies present in many other instruments that will only muddy the waters if they are all added to the mix. Could an electric guitar have frequencies present in the sub-bass range? Yes! Do I want the electric guitars competing for mix space with the bass guitar? Absolutely not! Enter the highpass filter...

When I mix, I place highpass filters on everything in the mix that doesn't need to be occupying the sub-bass frequency range. As you are mixing, decide what you want to "live" in the 20 to 80Hz area and filter out everything else that doesn't belong. Even if some instruments produce frequencies that you would normally want to occupy the sub-bass area, you may choose to filter them out for creative reasons. Just use your creativity while listening carefully, to prevent things from becoming too fat down on the bottom.

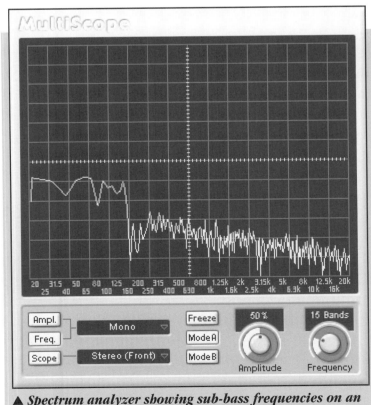

▲ *Spectrum analyzer showing sub-bass frequencies on an electric guitar before highpass filter is engaged.*

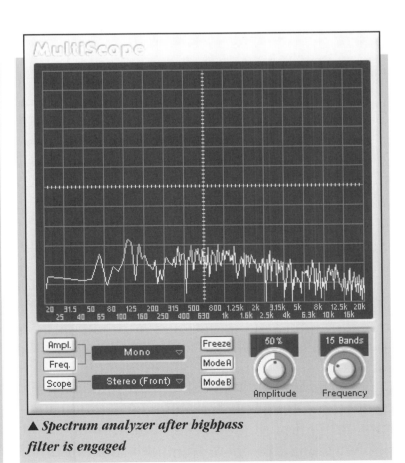

▲ *Spectrum analyzer after highpass filter is engaged*

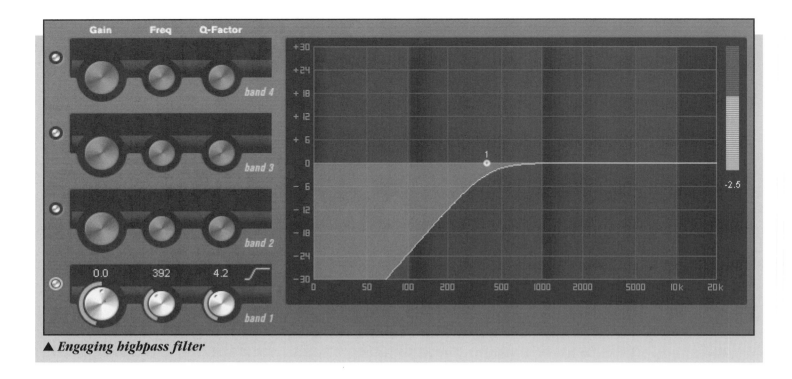

▲ *Engaging highpass filter*

The fundamental notes for most bass-producing instruments live in the 80 to 250Hz range. However, it can often seem like almost everything else in the mix is invading this range, which is why this frequency range is often a problem area for inexperienced mix engineers. Remove too much in this frequency range, and your mix will need too eat a few donuts because it will get too thin. Boosting too much or not removing enough frequency information in this area, however, will give your mix a nice set of love handles. You want your mix to be fit and full, but not fat and bloated.

As you listen to the song, decide which instrument(s) you want to feature in this frequency area. Insert a low-shelf EQ or a peak filter on anything extra that is muddying the waters. Listen closely and start carving out space until you are pleased with the balance in the bass frequencies. Remember not to make it too thin.

EQing the Low Mids

The low-mid range is from 250 to 400 Hz. This area can be problematic because almost every instrument and voice produces frequencies in this range. The result can be a muddy build-up that takes lots of practice to learn how to navigate. I even know a couple of mix engineers who start every mix with a peak filter cutting out a few dB at 300 Hz on every track!

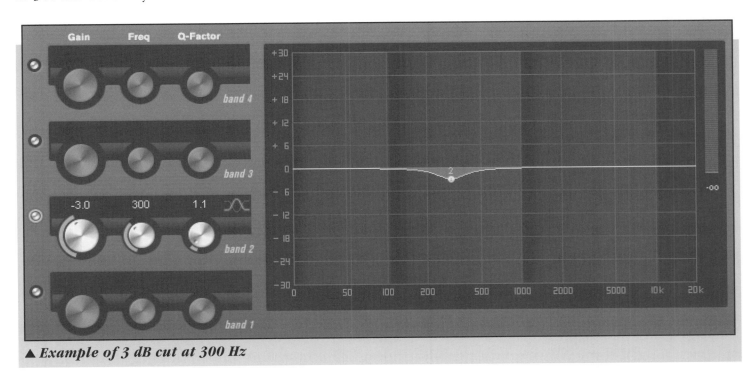

▲ *Example of 3 dB cut at 300 Hz*

Just like everything else in mixing, listening, listening, and more listening is at the heart of the EQ process. Insert a peak filter on every track and begin to boost the low mids on one track at a time. Listen to what happens to the perception of one instrument when you boost the low mids of another. Be very careful here; you can easily take out too much and make the mix sound thin, or leave too much in, making the mix muddy. You'll need to decide which elements need to be pronounced in the low-mid area and make room in the mix by cutting these frequencies in everything else that is getting in the way. Never completely eliminate all of the low mids of any instrument unless you've made a creative decision to do so—just a minor cut of 1 or 2 dB can make a world of difference.

EQing Mids and High Mids

Mids and high mids range from 400 to 6k Hz. This is the area where vocals live in the mix. The vocal is usually the focal point in the mix, so be sure to clear out enough space so stunning vocal performances will not get trampled on by other mix elements.

One good approach to beginning your mix is to listen to the lead vocal track alone. Turn everything else down and get the vocal EQ sounding great; then, add the other instruments, one at a time. As you are bringing in the rest of the instruments, listen to how they interact with the vocal. If you've ever been in a band, you know that most people, I mean instruments, have a hard time getting along with the lead vocal, but you'll need to try to keep peace in the mix. Try inserting a peak filter on each of the instruments that are getting in the way of the vocal and carve out the necessary frequencies so you don't have to turn up the vocal to make it audible.

The high mids are also the "ouch" area—or, as I like to call it, the "knife-in-the-forehead" area. I knew a live sound engineer who would give the singer a little extra 2 kHz in his monitors if he was being especially difficult that day; it usually calmed him right down. But, I digress…suffice to say, the 1 to 4 kHz range can really hurt the ears. The high mid frequency range, like all of the rest of the bands, requires a delicate balancing act to get correct. Experiment with mild to radical EQ changes in the high mids and listen to what each change does. Try using peak filters with an extremely high Q setting and a substantial gain decrease. Gradually lower the Q and listen to the way that affects the tonal shape of the signal. Now do the same with a gain increase. Almost all of the mid-range frequency balancing maneuvers can be handled by peak filters.

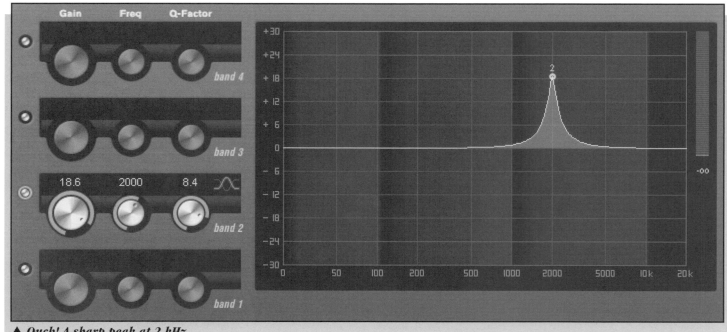

▲ *Ouch! A sharp peak at 2 kHz*

EQing the High End

The high end generally ranges from 6 to 20 kHz. The area ranging from 6 to 9 kHz is where most vocal sibilance is located. A brittle sounding mix can result from too much emphasis in the 8 to 16 kHz range.

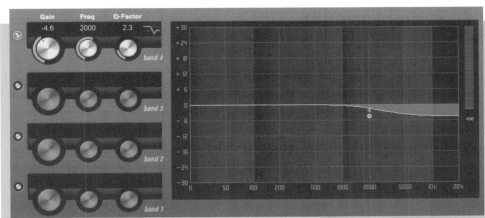

▲ *Make room for one source's high frequencies to come through by cutting the high frequencies on another, using a high-shelf filter.*

Getting high end correct involves cutting lower frequencies as much as it does boosting higher frequencies. Decide which elements of your mix need to be living in the high end. But rather than boosting the high end on those instruments, try inserting a high-shelf EQ on the instruments that don't need to be emphasized as much in the high-frequency range and start cutting. Using this approach will result in a more natural, less brittle high end. Having said that, there are instances where adding a touch of high end is just what the song needs, and in this situation, choosing the right EQ is very important. Poorly designed EQs really show their weaknesses when boosting high frequencies. So listen, listen, and listen some more. A/B your mix with commercial CDs with similar styles to check the entire frequency balance. Choosing EQs for each instrument and application takes lots of patience and lots of listening to determine which one will best suit the instrument, song, style, and your vision. Remember, there are no rules. Just use your ears—and if it sounds good, it is good!

 QUICK GUIDE

Instrument Frequency Ranges

This comparison of common rock band instruments and their frequency ranges will help you hone in EQ frequencies:

Kick Drum: Ranges from 40 to 8k Hz. Bottom end and punch range from 40 to 100 Hz, and "fullness" ranges from 100 to 250 Hz; ranges from 3 to 5 kHz.

Snare Drum: Ranges from 100 to 10k Hz. "Fatness" ranges from 120 to 250 Hz, attack ranges from 2 to 5 kHz, and brightness ranges from 7 to 10 kHz.

Toms: Range from 70 to 10k Hz. "Roundness" and low ring range from 80 to 150 Hz, attack ranges from 5 to 7 kHz.

Cymbals: Range from 200 to 18k Hz. "Harshness" ranges from 1 to 5 kHz, "shimmer" ranges from 10 to 18 kHz.

Bass: Ranges from 40 to 7k Hz. Bottom end and "punch" range from 40 to 85 Hz, "growl" ranges from 400 to 500 Hz, and "snap," or attack, ranges from 2 to 4 kHz.

Piano: Ranges from 20 Hz to 18k Hz. Piano tone covers this full range; it can get "honky" in the 2k Hz range.

Guitars: Ranges from 80 to 10k Hz. "Power" ranges from 250 to 500 Hz, "bite" and "edge" range from 2 to 6 kHz.

Vocals: Range from 80 to 16k Hz. "Warmth" ranges from 120 to 250 Hz, "power" ranges from 500 to 800 Hz, "presence" ranges from 2,000 to 4,500 Hz. Sibilance ranges from 5 to 9k Hz; "air" and breath sounds range from 12k Hz and above.

CHAPTER 4   DYNAMICS PROCESSORS

Compressors

What Are Compressors, and Why Would You Use One?

Compressors are devices that reduce the dynamic range of audio signals. In general terms, louder sounds over a defined threshold are reduced in level (compressed) while quieter sounds below the threshold are left unaffected. More simply put, a compressor is an automatic volume control. In addition to being used for general volume control, compressors are also used for more creative tasks such as tone control boxes, sibilance removers and distortion generators.

Types of Compressors

There are a huge number of analog and digital compressors available today. Digital compressors, like those used in digital audio workstations, use software algorithms to model the gain-control characteristics of analog compressors. Some programmers attempt to make an exact models of analog devices while others create completely new designs that take advantage of current computer technology to the fullest. I'm not going to get into great depth on the science behind various types of compressors; you need to use your ears and decide for yourself which compressor best suits your particular need. Also, I don't want to put you in a box by telling you a certain type of compressor is always best for certain things. While there is some truth to that, it's best for you to experiment as much as possible.

The Controls

Input Gain

Most compressors have a similar set of controls. Input gain is the amount of signal (audio) coming into the compressor before the signal is processed. The Input Gain control either increases or decreases the level of the signal coming into the compressor.

Threshold

The Threshold control sets the level where compression will kick in. It is usually measured in dB. If, for example, the threshold is set to -30 dB, each time the signal reaches -30 dB or more, it will be compressed. A lower Threshold setting will result in a larger portion of the overall audio signal being compressed; a higher Threshold setting will result in a smaller portion of the audio signal being compressed.

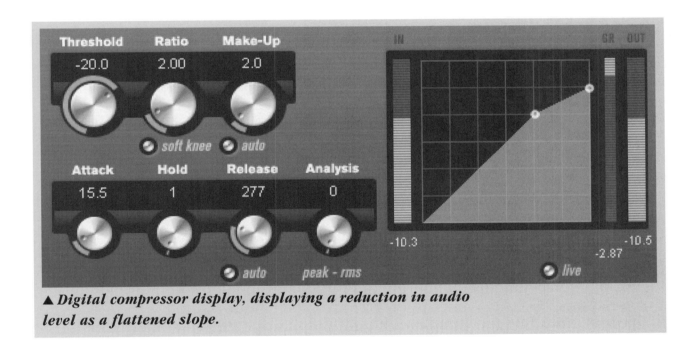

▲ *Digital compressor display, displaying a reduction in audio level as a flattened slope.*

Ratio

The Ratio determines the proportion of input to output above the threshold. For example, a 4:1 Ratio means that an input signal that is 4 dB above the Threshold would exit the compressor 1 dB above the threshold.

Attack

The Attack setting defines the length of time it takes the compressor to decrease the gain by the amount determined by the Ratio setting; a faster attack time means that the compressor will compress the signal more quickly than a slower attack time. Attack is often measured in milliseconds (ms).

Release

The Release setting refers the length of the time taken for the compressor to stop compressing, i.e. increase the gain back to zero dB of attenuation. The Release function kicks in once the input gain has fallen below the threshold. A faster release time means that the compressor will stop attenuating (reducing) the signal faster than if it were set to a slower release time.

Knee

The Knee setting refers to the response curve of the compressor. The Knee can typically be set for either Soft or Hard. A Soft Knee setting will slowly increase the compression ratio on a rounded curve as the level increases until the ratio setting is reached. A Hard Knee setting will apply a much sharper ratio response curve once the input level crosses the threshold.

Makeup Gain

Makeup Gain is an additional gain stage applied to the output of the compressor. Since compressors reduce the source signal, Makeup Gain is used to "make up" for the gain reduction during compression.

Compression vs. Limiting

Compression and limiting are the same process, but limiting is much more extreme as it generally refers to a compressor with a high ratio (often 10:1) and a fast attack time. "Brick wall" limiters have a very fast attack time and very high ratio and are generally used to prevent clipping (distortion caused by cutoff of a signal that is too loud).

Multiband Compressors

Multiband compressors differ from normal or single band compressors in that they split the input signal using crossovers (filters that separate audio signal) or bandpass filters into multiple frequency segments called bands. After the signal is split each frequency band has its own compressor with its own set of compression controls. (Band-pass filters are simply highpass and lowpass filters used together to filter out everything other than a specific frequency band.) A multiband compressor is often a good choice for vocals. The singer may have a particularly harsh frequency that comes out in his voice when he sings certain notes, or sections of a song. The multiband compressor can be set to isolate and compress the offensive frequency range, giving the vocal a more even frequency balance from section to section. Set the threshold correctly and the offensive areas will be ducked out of the way, leaving the rest of the vocal untouched.

▲ *Multiband compressor screen, demonstrating different levels of compression applied to different frequency bands. The top half of the screen shows the entire frequency range, and he bottom half displays each band separately.*

Sidechaining

Sidechaining is a process that uses the signal level of one source to control the compression level of a second source. I often use this method to adjust the relationship between the kick drum and the bass guitar. Many digital audio workstations have a built-in sidechain function; this is how I typically accomplish sidechain compression. For example, let's say I want to duck (reduce the level of) the bass guitar every time the kick drum hits; this a useful technique for creating a tighter, more solid feel between the kick drum and bass guitar. I insert a compressor into the signal path on the bass guitar, and activate its Key input—which tells the compressor to engage only when signal is present on the Key input. Then, I send the kick drum signal via an effects send to the key input on the bass guitar compressor. Set the appropriate settings on the bass guitar compressor and voila…sidechain compression.

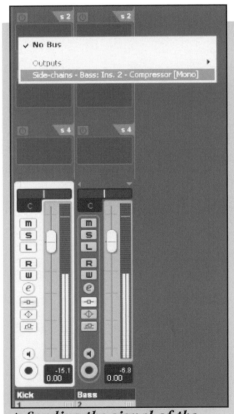

▲ *Sending the signal of the kick drum to the sidechain input of the bass guitar compressor. In this software compressor, the output is selected in a drop-down menu.*

▲ *Kick drum (note level meter on left) triggering the sidechain compressor on the bass guitar. Notice the lower meter level on the bass guitar track (next to the kick meter).*

Parallel Compression

In parallel compression, a compressor is inserted on a parallel signal path to the original. This technique leaves the dynamics untouched on the original track while adding low-level enhancement to the parallel compressed track, an approach commonly used on drums. An easy way to set parallel compression up on a snare drum track would be to simply copy the snare drum to a separate track, insert a compressor and the copied track, and adjust to taste. While mixing, simply blend the compressed track with the original until the desired effect is achieved.

▲ *An example of a parallel compressor applied to snare: Note the higher level on the original Snare track on the left meter, and the lower level on the Snare Copy track.*

Set up multitrack parallel compression through the use of aux sends
and buses or group tracks (configuring track output destinations and
combining tracks). Let's say you are working with 10 drum tracks.
First, assign the output of all 10 of those drum tracks to a single bus or
group track; I'll call this Drum Group 1. Next, set up a second bus or
group track and name it Drum Compressed 1. Now, set up aux sends
on each of the 10 drum tracks and the Drum Group 1 track, to send
their signals into Drum Compressed 1. Insert a compressor on Drum
Compressed 1. You can add as much of the 10 original drum tracks to
the Drum Compressed 1 track as you want by raising the level of the
aux sends, then adjust the compressor settings and fader level on the
Drum Compressed 1 track until you get the sound you're after. Use the
aux sends to send signals for processing, either from the original 10
tracks or the Drum Group 1 track, or a combination of all of them.

▲ *Parallel compression on a multitracked drum kit. Note level
meters for individual drum tracks, and for Drum Group and Drum
Compressor tracks.*

This technique is simply inserting two compressors in the signal path, one after the other. Typically, one compressor is used to control dynamic peaks and the other one is used to control the overall dynamic range. Combination compressors have a built-in serial compressor path, and they are usually referred to as compressor/limiters. These devices offer two dynamics processors; one is typically a fast-attack/fast-release limiter, and the other is a typical compressor. When done well, serial compression can sound very natural even when the source signal is heavily compressed.

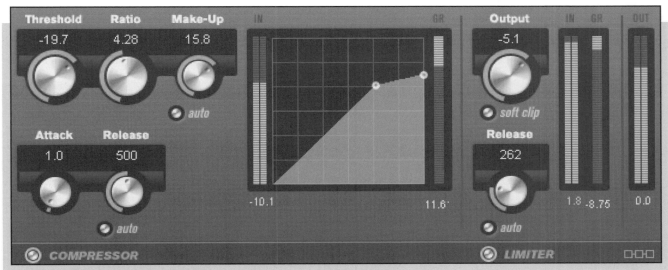

▲ *Compressor/limiter serial processor. Note the two sets of parameter controls.*

Compressors as Tone Devices

Due to their unique circuitry, many analog processors change the sound of a track as soon as they are added to the signal path, even if no actual compression is applied. Sometimes, all you want is a little "color," without any additional gain reduction. If that is the case, just insert the colored compressor and set the threshold high enough so that it never compresses the signal. A few compressors that are known to be colorful even when they are not set to alter dynamics are the Universal Audio LA2A, the Neve 33609, and the Tube-Tech CL1b. There are many more out there that have unique tonal benefits. Try inserting every compressor you have with the threshold turned all the way up and see if the tone of the source signal is altered in a pleasing way. This approach is a relatively easy way to shape your individual tracks and your mix.

Andy Johns is a prolific engineer and producer. Before his nineteenth birthday, he was working as Eddie Kramer's second engineer on classic recordings by Jimi Hendrix and many others. In a career spanning more than thirty years, he has engineered or produced records by artists ranging from Led Zeppelin and The Rolling Stones to Van Halen and Rod Stewart.

Courtesy Bobby Owsinski

Is Louder Better?

The mantra "louder is better" is true—if you're talking about a fire alarm. Some folks believe that "louder is better" is true as it relates to music, too. I don't! Louder might be better, or it might not—the appropriate level totally depends on the song, production style, and how the song is mixed.

Too many engineers try to make their mixes as loud as possible by over-compressing and over-limiting, at the expense of clarity, impact, and punch. This "louder is better" movement started as an attempt by engineers, producers, and record companies to make their songs stand out on the radio—the idea being that the listener would be drawn to the louder song more than the songs played before and after it, simply because it was louder.

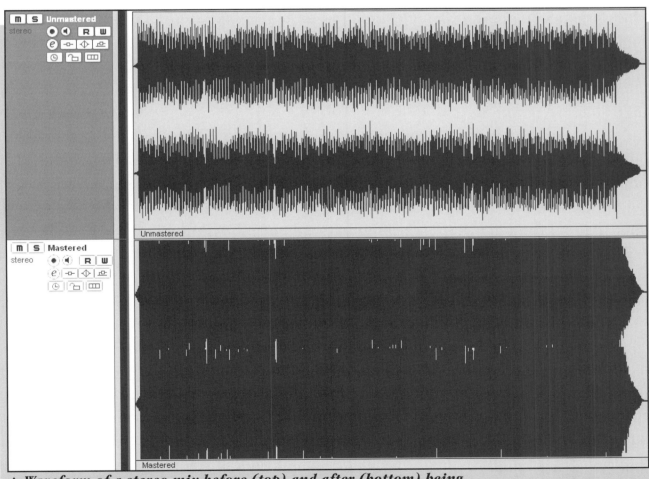

▲ *Waveform of a stereo mix before (top) and after (bottom) being squashed into oblivion—I mean, made louder. Note the lack of dynamic range in the bottom example.*

It is important to note that overuse of compression and/or limiting not only removes too much dynamic range, it can cause distortion and clipping; basically, it can destroy the life of the music. When referencing your mixes with commercial CDs, make sure you match the levels of the commercial releases with your mix—just turn down the CDs so there is no difference in perceived loudness between the two mixes. Focus on the sound, not the loudness.

I do understand the fight we are up against as mix engineers. Many producers and artists I have mixed projects for have made comments like, "I love the mix, but can you make it louder?" Or, "Why is this Green Day song so much louder than mine?" I try to educate my clients on the matter—sometimes it works, and sometimes it doesn't. I prefer more dynamics in my mixes. There have been times, however, when the client has wanted a louder mix, and I have given them what they want. But I will at least give them a choice between the two, so they can make an educated decision after hearing both.

My advice to you is, just make it sound good. Don't be overly concerned with making it louder. If the song feels like it needs more compression, compress it. If it doesn't, leave it alone.

Compressors In Use

Compressors are probably the most powerful and effective devices used to make a great mix. They are also the easiest processors to overuse and abuse. Compression will bring up the level of the noise floor so what may have been unnoticeable noise during recording suddenly becomes very apparent. But when used correctly, they can also make elements sit in just the right place in the mix. There is no right amount of compression, nor is there a "one size fits all" approach to compressor settings. After reading this section, spend lots of time experimenting. Do lots of listening to learn how compressors can enhance or degrade your mix.

Keep in mind that compressors and EQs need to work in tandem. The tonal shape of the source is going to most likely be different after compression is applied; also, changing an EQ setting that is inserted before the compressor is going to change how the compressor behaves. For example, if you apply a 10dB boost at 2,000 Hz on a vocal (why would anyone do that?), the compressor that is inserted after the EQ will be triggered by the massive boost at that frequency. Likewise, cutting frequencies before hitting the compressor will result in the compressor kicking in later than it otherwise would.

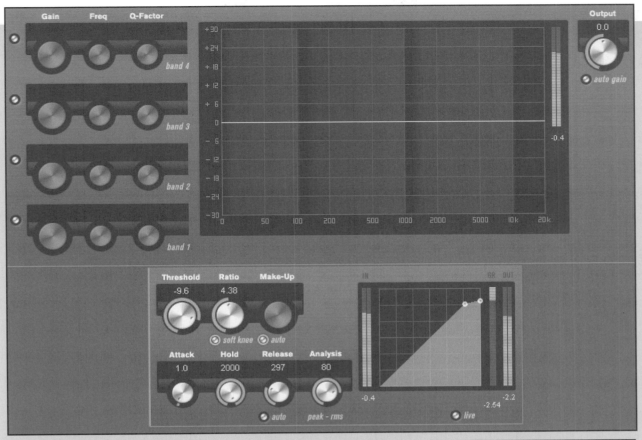

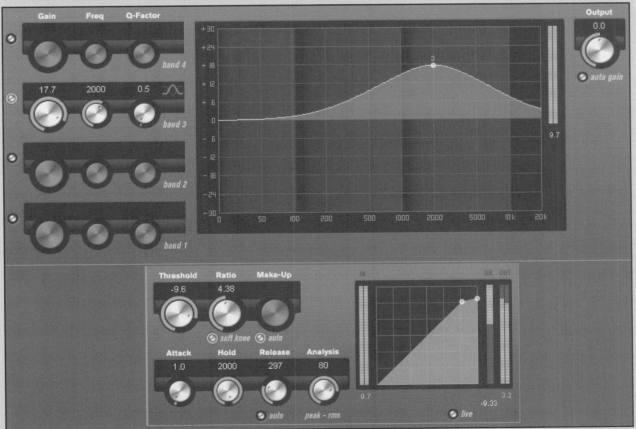

▲ *Examples of compressors with and without EQ boost inserted before them. Note the difference in gain reduction levels (in bottom right of each screen). Top: EQ inserted before the compressor without any boost; gain reduction is about 2.5 dB. Bottom: EQ inserted before the compressor, with a large boost at 2 kHz. Gain reduction is around 10 dB.*

Choosing a Compressor

There are no absolutes in deciding on which compressor you should use. You will tend to gravitate toward certain compressors for certain types of material, however. Some compressors just work better for material with fast attacks, such as drums, while others are better-suited for instruments with smaller dynamic ranges. As you begin to use the different types of compressors, the sound and of each type will become more obvious. As with EQs, the best thing to do is to try as many different compressors as you can and see which ones you like best in different situations. Remember, there are no rules; and if it sounds good, it is good!

The Sound of Compression

So now you know how compressors work. But how do they sound? Faster attack times are easier to hear than slower ones. Faster release times are more prone to "pumping" effects than slower release times. A Hard Knee setting is generally better suited for elements with sharper attacks like drums. Soft knee settings are generally better suited for sources like vocals where less obvious compression is required. Lower ratios with a slow attack and a quick release in combination with a high threshold yield the most transparent settings.

When you're first getting used to using compressors, it is a good idea to experiment with some radical settings so you can really hear how your compressors are functioning. As a starting point, insert a compressor on a snare drum track. Set a ratio of 4:1 with a Hard Knee setting. Set a very fast attack time, like 4 ms, and a very fast release time, like 10 ms. Take the threshold down to -40 so you can really hear the compressor working. Now experiment with changing the attack and release times. Notice that a slower attack time will allow more of the initial transient or attack of the snare drum to come through before the compressor kicks in.

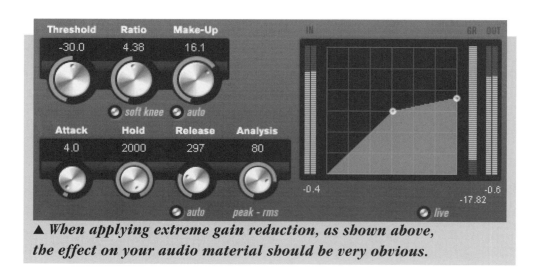

▲ *When applying extreme gain reduction, as shown above, the effect on your audio material should be very obvious.*

Try performing the same experiment on a wide variety of sources. Try it on vocals, acoustic guitars, and pianos, and use every compressor you have available. Setting a compressor's release time to pulse with the beat of the music is a great way to get satisfying compression on a mix. Since compressor release times are typically measured in milliseconds (ms), a chart or table that converts milliseconds to beats per minute (bpm) is a very handy resource to have.

A simple way to make your own chart is to use the following equation:

CONVERTING MILLISECONDS TO BEATS PER MINUTE

(QUICK GUIDE)

120,000/beats per minute=half-note value in ms

60,000/beats per minute=quarter-note value in ms

30,000/beats per minute=eighth-note value in ms

15,000/beats per minute=sixteenth-note value in ms

If your song tempo is 105 beats per minute and you wanted to find the release time that equaled eighth-notes at that tempo, the equation would look like this: 30,000/105 = 285.7 ms.

Also, don't forget to compensate for the gain reduction by applying makeup gain with the compressor. Experimentation is the best way to familiarize yourself with your tools. You have to be able to know what you have at your disposal and how it functions before you can use it effectively.

Compressing Instruments with a Wide Dynamic Range

Drum tracks typically have a very sharp attack that can, at times, be really hard to tame. There are a plethora (I wanted to use the word "plethora" at least once in this book) of approaches to compressing drums, and these approaches usually vary with different styles of music. In general, however, tighter drum sounds can be achieved by applying more compression with a shorter attack time. Again, be careful not to remove too much punch by going overboard.

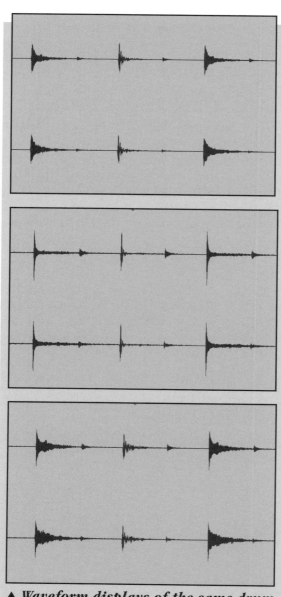

▲ *Waveform displays of the same drum track with three different compressor settings. Notice how the attack (transient) and sustain (tail) of each waveform is altered by different compressor settings.*

Try this experiment: Start with a kick drum track. Insert an EQ, followed by a compressor. I suggest choosing one with a fast attack, quick release, and a Hard Knee setting. Start with a 4:1 Ratio and a relatively slow attack (50 ms) and quick release (10 ms). Gradually bring the threshold down until you are noticing the sound of the compression and you are getting about 4 dB of gain reduction with each hit of the drum. Listen closely to the tone of the drum as the compressor is digging in. Now, go back to your EQ and gradually boost at 80 Hz until you have boosted 8 dB. Pay attention to the sound of the drum as that frequency boost triggers the compressor. Sweep the EQ up and down and listen to the way different frequency boosts interact with those compressor settings. Now, go to your EQ and bypass it for a moment. Gradually decrease the attack time and notice how that changes the sound of the kick drum. Slowly increase the release time, too. Now, adjust the ratio all the way up to 10:1.

The point of this exercise is to demonstrate the wide variety of sounds that can be achieved by changing the settings on a single compressor, and to demonstrate how EQ changes before compression can radically change the response of the compressor.

Another approach for dealing with wide dynamics is to use serial compression or a compressor/limiter combination. Try this: On the same kick drum channel, place a limiter or second compressor in the chain before the EQ and original compressor. Bypass the EQ and original compressor for the time being. Find the highest peak on the kick drum track and loop that section. The limiter should be set to Instant Attack (Use the Look Ahead option if there is one) and Fast Release. Set a ratio of 20:1 and lower the threshold so the signal is only attenuated a bit—no more than a dB or two. Now, take the original compressor and EQ out of Bypass and listen. (You'll need to adjust the settings of all three processors to get a desired sound.)

Experiment with a slightly lower attack time on the compressor/limiter to allow more punch and attack. The great thing about these different approaches is that there are no rules. You can experiment with any combination of limiters, compressors and EQs to get some great results. The key is to listen, know your tools and know what they can and can't do.

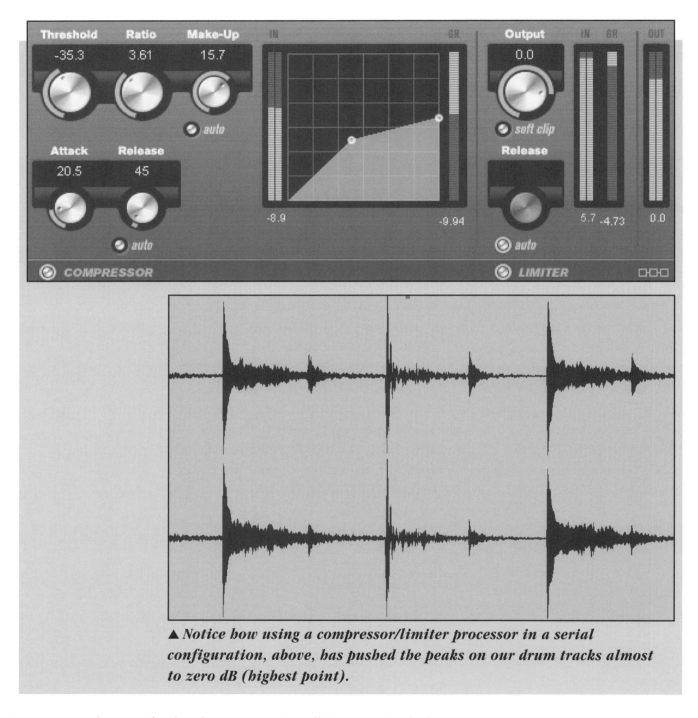

▲ *Notice how using a compressor/limiter processor in a serial configuration, above, has pushed the peaks on our drum tracks almost to zero dB (highest point).*

Other instruments that can be hard to get to sit well in a mix include acoustic guitars, percussion instruments, and horn sections. These instruments are all capable of very wide dynamic ranges, depending upon the type of performance. Experiment with multiple compressors in series and in combination with EQs. Change the order of the processors—don't get locked into doing the same thing every time.

Compressing Instruments with a Small Dynamic Range

A distorted electric guitar generally has a smaller dynamic range than other instruments. It may require less compression than other more percussive instruments—unless you're really going for an "in-your-face" type of effect where the guitars never move in the mix. But to demonstrate the effect of compression on electric guitar, I'll take a more moderate approach.

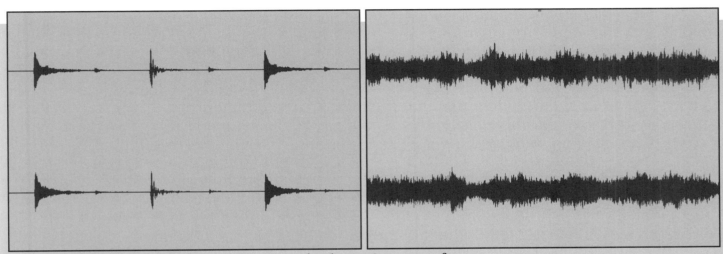

▲ *Notice the dramatic difference between the dynamic range of a drum kit (left) and a string pad (right). The drums have a much wider dynamic range, while the pad is much more static.*

Distorted electric guitars don't have big dynamic peaks because the circuitry and overdrive of the amp or other distortion processors used with them are already compressing the signal. In this exercise, the goal is to focus on the sustained notes of the instrument. First, try a slow attack and a mid to slow release with a 3:1 ratio. Adjust the threshold until you can hear the compressor working. Now, adjust the attack and release times until you are satisfied with the smoothness of the sustained notes. Depending upon the style of music and performance, you may want to take a much harder approach to compressing electrics. As a general rule, though, the smaller the range between the peaks and sustained notes of any instrument, the less you'll need to compress. The goal is to keep life in the music while making mix elements gel together. Use your ears and as you get more experienced, it will get easier.

Compressing Bass

Getting the bass part to have punch, clarity, and a solid feel throughout the song is one of the hardest things to pull off in mixing. Bass can be particularly challenging because it has both percussive attacks and long sustains; the goal is to get the attack and sustain to sound even and consistent. I find that serial compression works best for solving this problem (see graphics below).

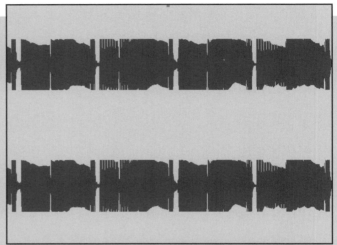

▲ *Bass track with a single compressor on slow attack.*

▲ *Bass with a limiter added in the chain with the compressor. Notice how attacks are more even with the sustains.*

The compression example I gave for kick drum also works well for bass. On bass, however, I almost always prefer using a compressor followed by a dedicated limiter, rather than two compressors. However, you can use two compressors effectively if one of them has fast enough attack and release times. A good starting place for bass is to set the first compressor for a relatively slow attack (30 ms) with a mid to slow release (80 to 200 ms). Try a ratio of 4:1, or even higher. With this compressor, we are focusing on the sustained notes of the instrument. You'll need to adjust the parameters based on the type of track and the performance to get the instrument to have a solid sustain. After you have the first compressor rocking, adjust the limiter so the attacks are smoothed out and relatively even when heard alongside the sustained notes. Bass usually gets quite a bit of compression in most mixes, so don't be afraid if the gain-reduction meters are compressing a lot. Just use your ears.

Compressing Vocals

Vocals are the focal point of most productions, regardless of genre. The melody and its delivery can make or break a song. As such, it is the job of the mix engineer to translate that melody and delivery in the best possible light. Some vocal performances have very wide dynamic ranges between sections, while others remain fairly even. For this reason, compressing vocals rarely works the same from song to song.

I always get the vocal sounding the best I can with EQ prior to applying compression. I'll remove any unwanted frequencies so they won't be accentuated by the compressor. After you get the vocal EQ right, insert a compressor. Like with every other instrument, some trial and error will be required to get the compression settings how you want them, but you can start with a 3:1 ratio, an attack of 15 ms, and a release of around 80 ms. This will allow the initial transient to pass through the compressor without being attenuated. Now, lower the threshold until you really hear the compressor working. Notice the effect it has on the tone of the vocal. Since most compressors have distinct sound, you may have to try different ones until you find one that has the "color" that brings out the best tone in the vocal. After you've found the right compressor for the right voice, begin experimenting with attack, release, ratio and threshold. In addition to listening for an evening of dynamics, pay close attention to the tonal changes in the vocal as more compression is applied.

It's common to use serial compression on vocals. Try an insert chain that consists of an EQ, followed by a compressor, then another EQ, then a second compressor, then a limiter. See illustration on page 42. The combination may sound extreme, but often, applying bits of compression with multiple compressors can create a more natural effect than a single compressor when applying the same amount of gain reduction. Try compressing 1 or 2 dB with each of the two compressors and the limiter. This type of serial technique can often make the vocal "sit up front" in the mix without sounding overcompressed.

▲ *Top screen: Vocal waveform before effect is applied. Middle screen: vocal after first compressor is applied; notice the difference in the waveform peaks. Bottom screen: vocal waveform after both the compressor and limiter have been applied. Notice that the peaks are now even in level.*

Multiband compressors are versatile tools for vocal processing; I use multiband compressors almost like an additional EQ on vocal tracks. There are times when a singer will shift registers, or sing with more intensity, and the tonal balance of his voice will dramatically change. The most obvious example is when a song verse is sung in a lower register, and when the chorus hits, so do the annoying upper-midrange frequencies. In this situation, just isolate the problematic frequency range—usually around 1 to 3 kHz—and set up your multiband compressor to treat that specific range during the parts of the song where it is a problem. Try setting the ratio to 2:1 with a very fast attack and very fast release. Then adjust the threshold until the aggravating frequencies are ducked out of the way and vocal tone sounds consistent from verse to chorus. This approach will work across the entire frequency range—not just upper mids or problem areas—and it is a wonderful way to smooth out the frequency spectrum of the vocal.

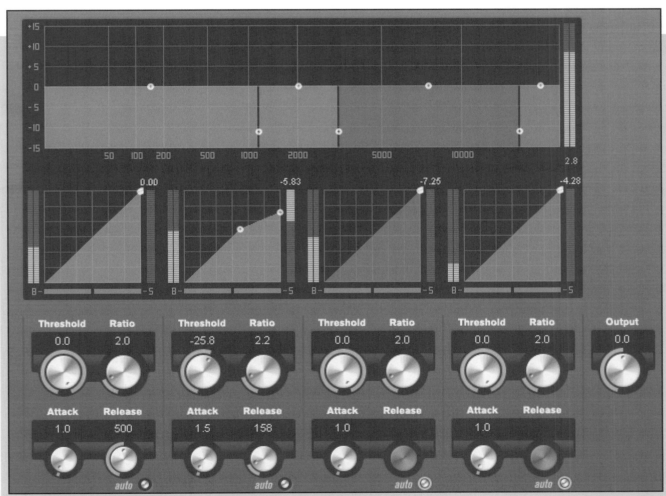

▲ *Multiband compressor set up to duck a specific frequency range (second curve from left) and leave everything else untouched.*

As you are working on the vocal, compare the compressed vocal to the original unprocessed track. If the vocal tone gets worse during compression, go back to the beginning and start over. If you are working in a digital environment, it is very easy to save your settings, so experiment with different insert chains on the same section of the song. Get three or four different set ups sounding as good as you can, then do an A/B comparison between them.

De-Essing

De-essing is the process of removing unwanted sibilance, or "ess" sounds, from a vocal performance. Ideally, your vocals would be recorded without extra sibilance, but some vocalists just sing with a very pronounced "sss" in their delivery, which often has to be dealt with during the mixing process. Factors such as compression, EQ, and limiting can also contribute to problem "ess" sounds. So, what can be done?

Method One:

A de-esser is a frequency-dependent compressor, which simply means that the compression function is keyed from a specific frequency. With most de-essers, the user can define the frequency that triggers the compressor; usually, the problem areas for vocal sibilance fall between 2 and 9 kHz. By inserting a de-esser in the vocal signal path and adjusting the parameters to grab the problem frequencies, you can effectively reduce sibilance. However, I typically don't like dedicated de-essers, because I can hear them working too much and the result just sounds unnatural to me. So what to do then?

▲ *An example of a dedicated de-esser,*
with minimal control parameters.

Method Two: Build Your Own De-Esser

Instead of inserting a de-esser on the vocal, I will sometimes create my own. Start by multing or copying the vocal onto three different tracks, and insert a highpass filter and lowpass filter on each of the three vocal tracks. Name vocal track #1 "vocal low/mid," vocal track #2 "vocal sss," and vocal track #3 "vocal high." Route each of the vocal tracks to a bus or group track, and name that track "vocal combined."

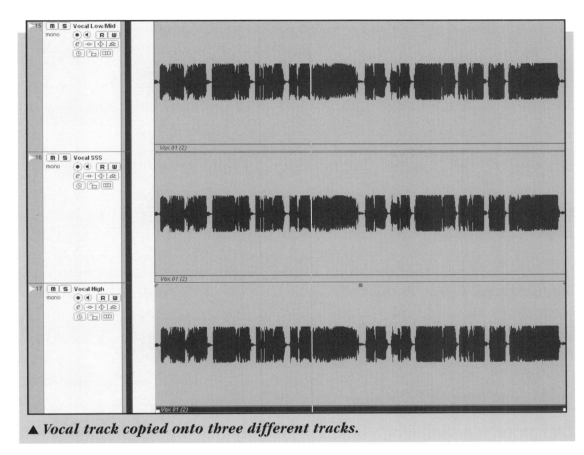

▲ *Vocal track copied onto three different tracks.*

On vocal track #1, set the highpass filter to 80 Hz and the lowpass filter to a frequency just below the problem sibilance area; I'd start at around 5 kHz. Listen to this track soloed (by itself), so you can hear the frequency point where the sibilance enters and becomes a problem. You want to be sure that no sibilance is present on this track.

On vocal track #2, isolate the sibilant frequencies using the highpass and lowpass filters. Try setting the highpass filter around 5 kHz and the lowpass filter around 7 kHz. Adjust these EQ points so you hone in on the problem area. Again, you will need to listen to this track soloed so you can hear the area of the vocal you are affecting.

On vocal track #3, only use the highpass filter. Set the filter so it rolls off the frequencies above the sibilance area, but keep the setting as close as possible the lowpass filter setting on vocal track #2.

Now set the fader levels of all three vocal tracks to unity or 0 dB and listen to make sure that when they are combined, the vocal still sounds natural. If it doesn't you may need to adjust the EQ on each of the three vocal tracks. After all three tracks are combined and sound natural, you will have a total of four faders for the lead vocal: "vocal low/mid," "vocal ess," "vocal high," and "vocal combined."

For compression, general EQ, and other effects, the approach here is to treat the "vocal combined" track as if it was your main lead vocal track; apply compressors or other insert effects to this track. Then, while mixing, you simply ride the "vocal ess" track up and down to minimize the sibilance in problem areas of the song. I know this may seem like a lot of work, but the result can be much more natural sounding than a dedicated de-esser. Remember that our job is to give the song the best treatment possible, and sometimes that means going the long way around for a ten-percent increase in quality. Speaking of the long way around...

Method Three: Chop and Cut

Method three is the technique I use most often, and it is the most time-consuming. This method will only work if you are working with a digital audio workstation with editing capabilities. If you're using analog tape you could try this using a razor blade on one of your two-inch reels but I wouldn't recommend it!

Start by creating a new audio track directly under your lead vocal track in your DAW, and name it "lead sibilance," or something similar. Solo the lead vocal and start playback. When you hear the first "sss," stop playback and zoom in on the lead vocal to the point where you can see the waveform where the "ess" is located. The "esses" are easy to visually identify because they are made up of high-frequency information. Thus, the waveforms are very close together, which makes them stand out from the rest of the lead vocal waveform. Now cut out the "ess" and drag it down to the newly created "lead sibilance" track. Go through the rest of the song, cutting out all of the sibilance and moving each piece to the sibilance track.

▲ *A DIY de-esser—notice the EQ filters on each of the three vocal tracks (faders 1–3), all assigned to "vocal combined" (fader 4).*

Be very careful, when moving the sibilant pieces to the new track, not to shift them either before or after the places where they originally occurred in the timeline. I will sometimes edit other sounds such as "f"s, "k"s, "c"s, and "d"s onto the sibilance track, because these sounds can also cause sibilance problems. After you have performed all of the edits, put very short fade-ins and fade-outs on all the edits on both vocal tracks.

Now, insert a highpass filter on the sibilance track and roll off everything below 900 Hz. It is important to do this because there is often unwanted air movement before the "esses." Route each of the vocal tracks to a bus or group track and name it something like "lead vocal combined."

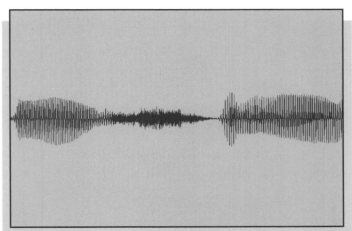

▲ *Waveform of a vocal track—notice how easy the sibilant frequencies are to identify. This sibilance occurs between two larger waveforms.*

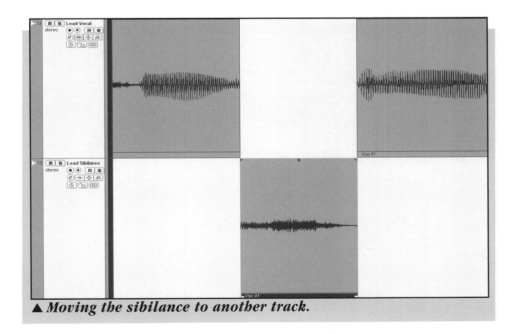

▲ *Moving the sibilance to another track.*

In this exercise, I treat the original lead vocal track as my main vocal track for compression and other effects while leaving the sibilant track au naturale. A very nice side effect of using this method is that you can add huge high-frequency boosts to the lead vocal and make it as "airy" as you want without it getting too sibilant because all the sibilance is on a separate track! As you mix the song, just ride the fader on the sibilance track so the level of the "ess" sounds stay consistent.

Bus Compression

Bus compression is simply applying compression to a group of instruments at the same time, by sending the outputs of those instruments to the same group track or bus track. Bus compression can be applied to just two or three instruments or the entire stereo mix.

A common use for bus compression during the mixing is on the drum bus. Drum bus compression can make the drum kit gel or glue together and add punch to the drums. To set it up, send the output of all your drum tracks to the same group track or bus and insert a compressor on that group track. Keep in mind that when using bus compression, the compressor's settings are affecting all the tracks in that group. So if the fader is turned up on the kick drum, the kick drum will hit the compressor harder, thus changing the way the bus compressor interacts with the rest of the drums. Using bus compression this way can make your mix punchy and exciting but, as with all compression, care should be taken to not go too far and remove the life and all dynamics from the music.

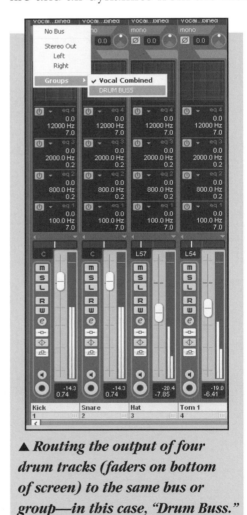

▲ *Routing the output of four drum tracks (faders on bottom of screen) to the same bus or group—in this case, "Drum Buss."*

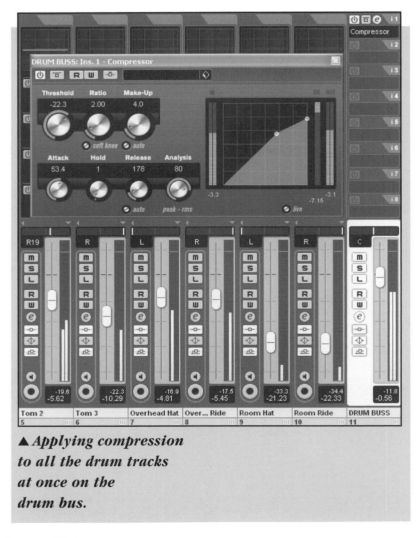

▲ *Applying compression to all the drum tracks at once on the drum bus.*

Bus compression is by no means limited to drums. If there are a limited number of compressors in your studio, bus compression can be used to combine similar tracks and apply compression to all of them at once.

Background vocals can benefit from bus compression. If you're mixing a song with 16 tracks of background vocals, you could either treat them as 16 individual tracks or as a stereo group. Set this bus up the same way you set up drum bus compression: Route the outputs of the background vocal tracks to the same group track or bus. Insert a compressor on the group track and compress to taste. For me, the main difference between applying bus compression on background vocals versus a drum bus is philosophical. I view drum bus compression technique as more of an effect, whereas I view the background vocals technique more as a way to save on resources as well as providing a way to be able to mix faster by only having to set up one compressor. Remember, the only rule is to be creative and make it sound as good as you can.

Stereo mix bus compression is the process of compressing the entire stereo mix by inserting a stereo compressor on the stereo mix bus or master fader. There are differing opinions on whether or not to compress the stereo mix before mastering. Some take the approach that the mastering engineer shouldn't have to do anything with the final mix other than put the songs in the correct sequence and burn the final CD. Others believe that the stereo mix should be completely free of dynamics processing (no compression) and let the mastering engineer take care of it. Still other mix engineers fall somewhere in between, applying stereo mix compression if they think some is needed. Regardless of which camp you fall into, you should understand stereo mix compression.

Some engineers prefer to mix into the stereo mix compressor from the start of the mix process, while others like to add it at the end. Others take a hybrid approach by checking the mix with and without compression, by frequently bypassing the compressor at various times throughout the mix. To mix into a stereo mix compressor, you'll need to insert one on the stereo bus from the very beginning of the process before you add any EQ or compression to any of the individual tracks. The idea here is that the choices made during the mixing process should be made while listening through the compressor, since the intent is to ultimately keep it in the signal path. By letting the compressor color the sound from the beginning, you'll make better choices along the way than if you just add the compressor after you have finished the mix.

Stereo mix compression can act as glue. It can give your mix a sense of being "held together," and it can add punch and impact. But when taken too far, it can totally suck the life out of a mix. As a general rule, applying slower attack times and quicker release times will result in less noticeable stereo mix compression. A low ratio and Soft Knee setting will also result in more transparent mix bus compression. However, certain styles of music can definitely benefit from a harder Knee and a fair amount of stereo mix compression.

Other Creative Compression

Applying multiple parallel compressors can be an effective way to enhance a mix. One really cool trick is to set up different compressors for different frequency ranges in a mix. I approach this two different ways.

Method One

The first approach is to set up three new buses—one to process each frequency range—and insert a compressor on each. Make sure that each compressor is different. This is when knowing your tools becomes very important, because each compressor is going to be used to process a different element in the mix, based on the frequency ranges the instruments occupy and the way the three compressors interact with those frequencies. If you have a compressor that works particularly well on low-frequency material, such as kick drum and bass guitar, use that one on one of the three buses. Choose another compressor that has a nice midrange color to it, and insert that one on the second bus. Finally, insert a compressor that you like to use on high-frequency material on the third bus.

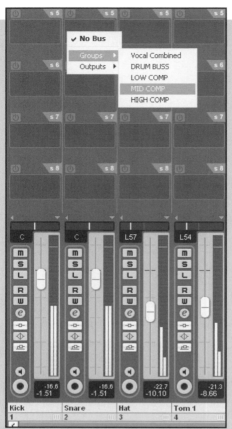

▲ *First, the snare drum track (fader 2) is sent to the mid-frequency (MID COMP) parallel compressor, using an aux send.*

Next, you'll need to decide which instruments to send into each of the three parallel compressors. As a starting point, decide which instruments are predominant in each of the three general frequency areas. Remember that there are no hard and fast rules, so experiment with different options. You may send some instruments into all three of the compressors, while some instruments might not need any compression at all. Experiment and see what works best for the song.

While mixing, use aux sends to send varying levels of all low-frequency instruments into the first parallel compressor bus, midrange instruments into the second, and all high-frequency material to the third. Set up the aux sends on the individual tracks to "pre-fader" if you want the level of the tracks going into the parallel compressors to change while you

▲ *The snare's signal is then sent to the stereo output, routed through the MID COMP parallel compressor which is also being sent to the stereo output.*

ride the faders; set them to "post-fader" to send a fixed level into the parallel compressors. As you mix, adjust the fader balances of the individual tracks and the parallel compressor tracks throughout the mix. If more low end is needed in the mix, boost the fader assigned to the low-frequency compressor. If more high end or mid range is needed, raise their respective faders. I will usually set these parallel compressors 20 dB lower than the stereo mix fader as a starting point. Try inserting an EQ either before or after each of the parallel compressors to further shape the tonal balance of your mix. You get the idea!

Method Two

Using this method, you will build your own parallel multiband compressor. To pull this off, first set up six group tracks or buses. Bus #1 will be your mix bus; everything in the mix is routed to bus #1. Bus #2 will be the low-frequency compressor, bus #3 will be the low-mid-frequency compressor, bus #4 will be the mid-frequency compressor, bus #5 will be the high-mid-frequency compressor, and bus #6 will be the high frequency compressor. Unlike in approach #1, in which parallel compressors compress the full range of the instruments sent to them, using approach #2, you'll will filter out all unwanted frequencies before any signals hit the compressor. Then, the individual compressors will only compress the specific frequency content you've determined.

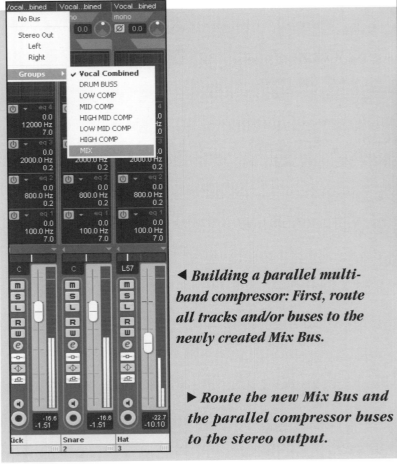

◀ *Building a parallel multi-band compressor: First, route all tracks and/or buses to the newly created Mix Bus.*

▶ *Route the new Mix Bus and the parallel compressor buses to the stereo output.*

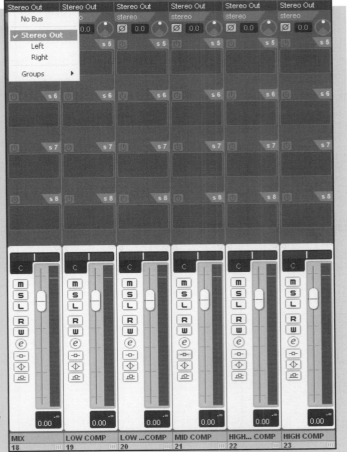

Next, on bus #1, set up a post-fader aux send into each of the five parallel compressor buses and set the level to Unity or 0 dB. On each of the five remaining buses, insert highpass and lowpass filters as the first processors in the insert chain. You should now have your entire mix routed to each of the five parallel buses, and buses 2 through 6 should have highpass and lowpass filters as the first insert in each path.

Next, dial in a good balance and rough mix. Pull the faders on buses 2 through 6 all the way down while you are getting this rough mix. After you feel good about your rough mix, bring up the fader on bus #2 and solo this bus so it is the only thing you are hearing. Be sure that your console or DAW (digital audio workstation) routing is set up so that soloing this bus will not also solo the mix bus fader you created. To achieve this, you may need to switch the sends for bus #1 to pre-fader and turn its fader down. The bottom line is, you'll need to hear buses 2 through 6 in solo mode while you are setting this up. You can switch the sends back to post-fader after the EQ filters and compressors have been set up if you need to.

Now, bus #2 is in solo. Use the lowpass filter to take out everything but the low-frequency information that you want to compress; I usually set this filter to roll off around 100 Hz. Adjust your settings while listening, so you can hear which elements of the mix remain audible and which are compressed by your low-frequency compressor. Then, set the highpass filter to roll off at 40 Hz. Now you have a bandpass filter, and the only audible frequencies on bus #2 are between 40 and 100 Hz.

Next, insert a compressor on bus #2 after the high and lowpass filters. This compressor's parameters will vary depending upon the program material. Listen to the attack and sustain of the notes that fall in this range, and adjust the compressor so you are getting plenty of punch and sustain. Keep in mind that the compressor settings will need to be adjusted again once you hear all the buses working together with the main mix bus. So for now, just get it in the ballpark.

Move on to the remaining buses, repeating the same set-up process. Configure bandpass filters on each of the buses so you are only hearing the parts of the mix you want to compress on that particular bus. Set up each compressor so it suits that particular frequency range, keeping in mind that you will probably need to tweak the settings later. After bandpass filters and compressors have been set up on all of the buses, turn down the faders for buses 2 through 6. (Take them out of Solo mode if you haven't already done that.)

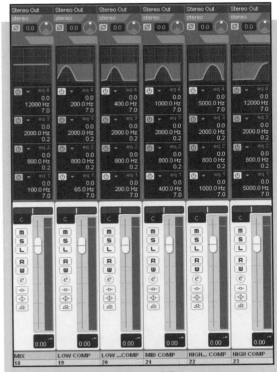

▲ Set all the high and lowpass filters on each of the parallel buses. Note filter curves at the top of each channel fader.

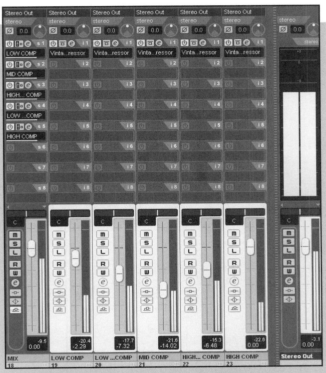

▲ Here the Mix Bus (leftmost fader) is using aux sends to feed the five parallel compressors, which are all being routed to the stereo output (rightmost fader).

At this point, you should have routed all of your individual audio tracks to bus #1, and buses 2 through six should be turned all the way down. Now, gradually turn up the faders for buses 2 through 6; pay careful attention to the effect each of the buses has on the sound of the mix as you blend them in. You can easily adjust the frequency balance throughout the mix by adjusting the fader balance of the parallel mix buses. You can even insert another compressor on the stereo output for a little more glue and/or color.

Keep in mind that there are as many "right" ways to compress something as you can dream up. When deciding on a compression approach, it is important to have an idea of the effect you are trying to achieve and know how to get there. So learn the capabilities, strengths, and weaknesses of your tools, keep experimenting, and come up with your own unique ways of using compression in your mixes.

Expanders

What Are Expanders, and Why Would You Use One?

I am writing this book around the Christmas season, and I know that one thing that keeps expanding right now is my mid section. Maybe I should develop a personal mid section compressor to take care of my expansion.... Anyway, audio expanders expand the dynamic content of an audio signal. In other words, they are the opposite of compressors. The most common uses for expanders are eliminating noise and adding dynamics to overly compressed audio material. Expanders basically make the quiet sounds quieter and the loud sounds louder. The controls on an expander are almost identical to those on a compressor.

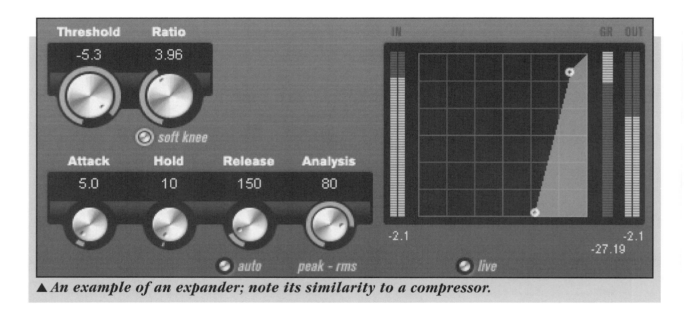

▲ *An example of an expander; note its similarity to a compressor.*

The Controls

Threshold

Compression takes effect when audio signal rises above a level threshold. An expander works in reverse: Expansion begins when the signal falls below a threshold, and only those signals falling below the threshold are affected.

Ratio

The Ratio setting determines the proportion of downward gain applied to the signal set below the threshold. For example, if the ratio is set to 2:1, any signal falling 3 dB below the threshold will be lowered to 6 dB below the threshold.

Attack

The Attack setting refers to the length of time it takes for the expander to process the signal once it falls below the threshold. A faster attack time means that the expander will process the signal more quickly than a slower attack time.

Release

The Release setting refers the length of the time it takes for the gain to return to its original level after the signal rises above the threshold.

Knee

The Knee setting refers to the response curve of the expander. The Knee can typically be set for either soft or hard. A Soft Knee setting will gradually increase the downward expansion ratio as the level increases until the ratio setting is reached. A Hard Knee setting is just that, hard; this setting will apply the full ratio set by the user once the input level is below the threshold.

Expanders In Use

Applications for expanders have changed dramatically over the years. Originally, expanders were primarily used in broadcast applications. Today, expanders are creative tools in the engineer's tool belt. If you receive overly compressed, lifeless tracks, expanders can be used to try to impart some energy back into them. As an experiment, try using a compressor to squash the life of a stereo mix. Then, insert an expander and see how much of the original dynamic range you can restore.

Noise Gates

What Are Noise Gates, and Why Would You Use One?

Noise gates are like automated Mute buttons. (I've had some conversations in which I wish I could insert an automatic Mute button on some folks, but unfortunately that technology isn't quite ready yet.) Noise gates are expanders taken to the extreme. When incoming signal falls below the specified threshold, the gate is closed—no signal passes through. When the signal is above the specified threshold, the gate is open—signal passes through the gate. Before the proliferation of digital audio workstations, noise gates were more heavily relied on, to keep certain elements from adding unwanted noise to the mix. Gates were commonly used on toms, for example, to keep out the "ringing" sounds they make while the rest of the kit is played. Today, you can easily achieve the same results in your workstation by editing out the noise on the tom tracks and just leaving the tom hits. This is not to say that noise gates are not used anymore; I'm just pointing out that technology will always change the way we use our tools to get our desired results. Other common uses for noise gates include removing room ambience in between lines on vocal tracks, or creating special halting effects with instruments, voices and reverbs.

▲ *Example of a noise gate. Note that many settings are similar to expander settings.*

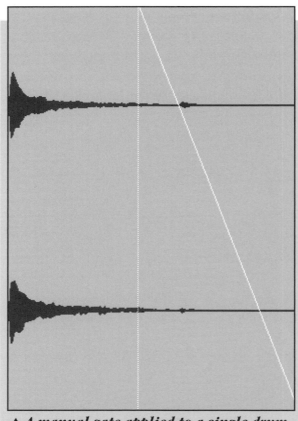

▲ *A manual gate applied to a single drum hit. All extraneous noise before and after the hit is removed through editing.*

The Controls

Threshold

The Threshold control follows the same principle as it does on a compressor; all signals falling below the threshold will be muted or heavily attenuated, and all signals crossing above the threshold will be passed through the gate with no attenuation.

Attack

The Attack setting adjusts the amount of time it takes the gate to open once it has been triggered by an audio signal passing the threshold.

Release

The release setting adjusts the length of time it takes the gate to close once the audio signal falls below the threshold.

Some noise gates feature additional controls such as Range, Hold Time and Sidechain. These can be useful in further fine-tuning how the noise gate is triggered and the way it responds after it has been triggered. For example, Sidechain can set the gate to be triggered by another audio track or a specific frequency; Hold Time can force the gate to stay open for a specific amount of time before the Release setting takes effect.

Noise Gates In Use

In mixing, the most common use for noise gates is simply inserting one into the signal path of an audio track and setting the parameters to eliminate unwanted noise. (For this reason, gates are usually inserted as the first device in the chain.) Another common technique is timing the gate release with the tempo of the song to produce rhythmic pulses in sync with percussive instruments. There are many ways to use noise gates creatively to help your mix to stand out. Use your imagination, and if you can dream it up, give it a shot!

CHAPTER 5 · SPACE: REVERBS, DELAYS, ETC.

Reverb

What is Reverb, and Why Do I Need It?

I know what a verb is, but reverb? Is reverb substituting one verb for another, or adding an extra verb to your sentence? Or, is the English language full of nonsense? I choose the latter! But back to the topic at hand…

If you've ever stood in an empty gymnasium or church and clapped your hands, you've heard reverb. Reverb, short for reverberation, is simply the persistence of sound in a particular space after the original sound has stopped. Reverb is created when a sound is produced in an enclosed space, bouncing around and causing reflections (echoes) to build up and slowly decay as the sound is eventually absorbed into the air, walls, or other surfaces.

In the recording process, the acoustic space where the instruments are recorded is critical to the overall sound of the instrument. A well-designed acoustic space will yield an amazing-sounding, naturally ambient recording, which will give space, dimension and life to the final mix. At times, however, your source tracks might need help in the ambience department. This is where reverb processors come into the mix, so to speak.

Reverb is time-based processing, vs. frequency-based (EQ) or level-based (compression) processing. Reverb can be used for adding a natural-sounding space to your individual tracks, for wacky special effects, or for making things sound "farther away" in

▲ *Studio D at Blackbird recording studio in Nashville, Tenn. Notice the variety of wall surface materials, which control and augment reflections in the room.*

the mix. There are many different types of reverb processors, including plates, rooms, spring reverbs, and convolution reverbs. (I'll explain all of these below.) Many commercial mixing studios have dedicated analog reverb units. In the not-too-distant past, using these types of units was the only way to get quality sounding reverb while mixing. Today however, there are scads of high-quality reverb software plug-ins available for use with digital audio workstations. Whether you are using computers or an old-school dedicated plate reverb, the concepts and controls apply for both.

The Controls

Different reverbs have different parameters—some have many options to tweak, while others may have just two or three. We'll take a look at six common parameters:

Predelay

Pre-delay sets the length of time between the original dry signal and audible beginning of the reverb.

Reverb Time

Reverb Time sets the time required for the reverb reflection level to decay to a level 60 dB lower than the direct (original) sound.

Reverb Size

This setting alters the delay times of early reflections to simulate larger or smaller physical spaces

Diffusion

Diffusion emulates the acoustic behavior of various types of surface materials in a room, such as brick walls or a carpeted floor.

Early Reflections

Early reflections are the first few "bounces" off the walls, floors, or ceiling that occur after the original sound is generated. These reflections give our brains the impression of room size and dimension, and in artificial reverbs, they are very important factors in our perception of space.

Mix

This controls the blend of dry (unprocessed) signal to wet (processed) signal.

▲ *An example of a reverb featuring basic controls, plus EQ adjustments and envelope-shaping capabilities.*

Types of Reverbs

Plates

A plate reverb happens when someone drops their dishes in a crowded cafeteria and everyone in the room makes that "ooh" sound... Not! Actually, a plate reverb uses an electromechanical transducer to create a vibration on a sheet of metal. A pickup captures the vibrations as they pass across the sheet, and those vibrations are output as an audio signal. Plates are not digital devices, but there many digital signal processors that mimic the sound of plate reverbs.

Springs

Springs are actually...springs! Similar to plates, spring reverbs use a transducer on one end of a spring and a pickup on the other. The pickup captures the vibrations of the spring and puts out an audio signal of those vibrations.

Rooms

This one is actually really simple: Room reverbs recreate the acoustics of actual spaces with walls, a floor and a ceiling. These spaces can be churches, halls, clubs, living rooms, bathrooms etc. Years ago, you would have to play a sound through a speaker in a room and re-record the sound of the room with a microphone to use a natural room reverb. Today, digital signal processors use computer algorithms to create the sound of a wide variety of rooms.

Convolution

Convolution reverbs use a mathematical convolution operation to process a pre-recorded impulse response of a physical or virtual space. These types of reverbs can sound like virtually any other reverb, or any acoustic space in existence. Does that sound convoluted?

Reverbs In Use

Normally, you'll only apply a few reverbs to a mix and route multiple instruments through those reverbs. The rationale behind using a just few reverbs for the entire mix, rather than a different reverb on every track, is to give the tracks some cohesion and to save on resources. It makes sense to make many instruments sound like they are in the same space, to give the mix a natural, glued-together effect. Configure track reverbs through effects sends and returns; most analog and digital mixing consoles have a few dedicated effects sends/returns and/or auxiliary sends/returns. If you are working on a computer-based workstation, these can be set up easily, simply by creating the necessary tracks.

Ready to try it out? Start by inserting a reverb on an auxiliary channel. Then, use an aux or effects send on each audio channel to send its signal to the auxiliary channel where the reverb is inserted.

Typically, these aux sends will be configured as post-fader, meaning that the signal going to the reverb channel will be adjusted in direct relationship to the changes made on that channel's fader. For example, say you have a lead vocal track with its fader set to 0 dB, or unity. You also have an aux send on that lead vocal track set to 0 dB, and it is routed to a reverb. Now, the level of the lead vocal signal going into the reverb is 0 dB, but if you lower the lead vocal fader to -10 dB, then the signal level of the vocal being sent via the aux send into the reverb will also be -10 dB. Changing the aux send to pre-fader simply means the aux send level will remain constant regardless of changes made to the channel fader.

When using the send/return method for reverb effects, you will generally set the reverb mix balance to 100% wet; this way, the output of the reverb includes none of the dry signal. This configuration is useful because most of the time you don't want the reverb send level to affect the overall volume of the track in the mix; you just want to hear the output of the reverb itself.

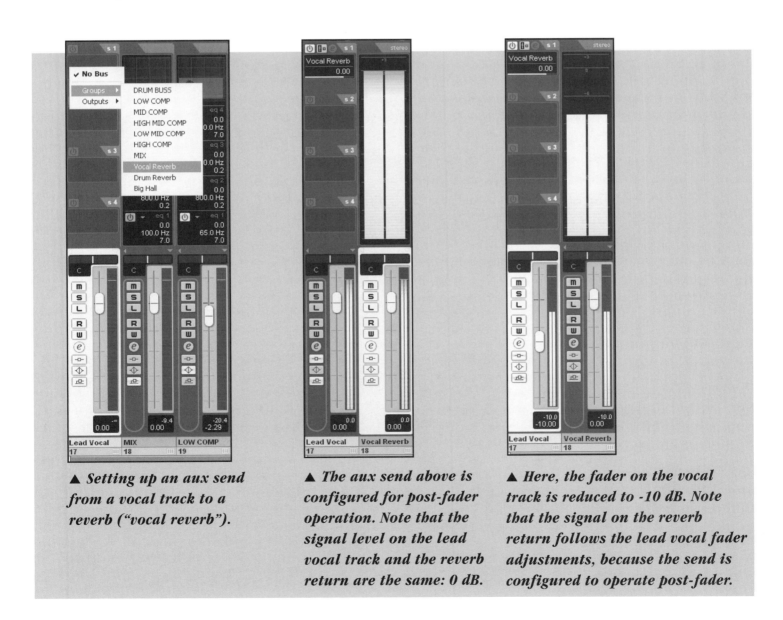

▲ Setting up an aux send from a vocal track to a reverb ("vocal reverb").

▲ The aux send above is configured for post-fader operation. Note that the signal level on the lead vocal track and the reverb return are the same: 0 dB.

▲ Here, the fader on the vocal track is reduced to -10 dB. Note that the signal on the reverb return follows the lead vocal fader adjustments, because the send is configured to operate post-fader.

Choosing a Reverb

Because there are so many reverb choices on the market today, it can be a very daunting task to decide which ones to use, and why to use them. While there are many reference resources available online and in print, the best way to familiarize yourself with the various reverb effects is plain old listening. But what should you listen for? This is where your creativity enters the picture. Take your time and imagine the type of space you hear for the song you are mixing. Is it the same space for every instrument and voice, or do you hear many different spaces? Listening through presets that are included with most reverbs is always a great place to start. But try to ignore the preset names, so you don't end up dismissing a preset on name alone without listening to it. Don't hurry through this process, because it is a critical step in honing in on a direction for the mix.

If you are new to mixing or are having a bit of trouble deciding on a reverb approach, don't worry—I'm here to help! Try this technique: Rather than start with just one reverb, start with two. We'll set up the first one to give the individual tracks cohesion; the second one will provide a more obvious sense of space, and you will be able to hear it more in the track.

For the first reverb that is intended to provide ambience rather than obvious "roominess," start with a Small Room or Small Hall setting. (Convolution reverbs work very well here, since they actually sample an acoustic space.) The reverb should have a short reverb time—the specific time is really dependent on the song, but a good starting point is around 500 ms. The pre-delay should also be short—around 10 ms. Try sending your snare drum, toms, electric guitars, pianos, and acoustic instruments to this reverb. Notice how the previously disconnected tracks start to blend better without sounding like they have an obvious effect on them. Adjust the send levels on each of the tracks until you have a nice gluing effect, without obvious reverb. You can also adjust the reverb return by raising and lowering the fader of the reverb effects track. Experiment with various reverb algorithms and settings to hear the effect each has on your mix. Make your own presets while you are experimenting so you can easily compare different reverbs.

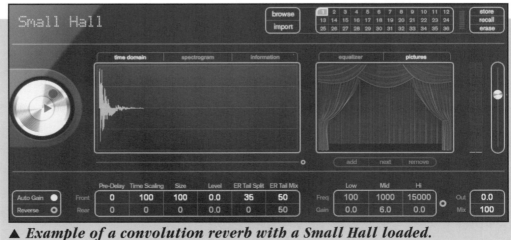

▲ *Example of a convolution reverb with a Small Hall loaded.*

The second reverb is intended to be more obvious. Where the first reverb is intended to gel mix elements together, this one is intended to give the listener a much bigger sense of space. Select a large hall for this exercise; set a long reverb time of three or four seconds and a very long pre-delay of 50 to 70 ms. Now, route something percussive like a snare drum through this reverb and begin adjusting the pre-delay time. Notice how your perception of the space changes as you adjust the pre-delay. Next, adjust the room size. The creative possibilities are truly endless here, which is why it is so important to have a general idea of how you want things to sound before you start. Your reverb decision is a creative choice; there are no right or wrong choices regarding which type to choose, or how much to use. Let your ears be your guide, and if it sounds good, it is good!

▲ *Large Hall reverb setting; note "reverb character" settings.*

Incorporating EQ and Other Processing

On almost every one of my mixes, I will add EQ or some other type of effect to the reverb return. There are many reasons to combine processors. Sometimes, the reverb will be the right room size and type, but will make the audio sound bit too bright or brittle. A simple solution is to insert an EQ after the reverb output, turn on a high-shelving filter and cut out the unwanted frequencies. There are also times where the material will become too muddy or boomy and require some low-frequency adjustments. Many reverb plug-ins and hardware units have built-in EQ controls. Remember to do comparative listening with and without the reverb in the mix to hear how the processing is affecting the sound quality of the tracks passing through it.

Other effect processors may also come in handy at times. A common effect in the '80s was to insert a noise gate after the output of the reverb, which would result in creating an abrupt halt on the tail of the reverb. Compression can also be used to shape the sustain of the reverb tail for an interesting effect. I have even placed reverbs after reverbs in serial fashion so the output of one is feeding the input of the other. As with all aspects of mixing, use your creativity to find the best choice for each mix.

How Much is Too Much?

There is no rule that says that a mix slathered (I love saying "slathered") with tons of reverb has too much. However, you might have a hard time getting many people to like a mix like that. You, the producer and the artist, will decide how much reverb to use, but you should keep a few guidelines in mind while you're mixing.

Small-room or ambience-type reverbs are intended to be noticed only when they're removed. If you are hearing the reverb tail or pre-delay on these in the context of the mix then you are probably using too much. As years pass trends and styles change. So use whatever you think works but keep in mind that with too much reverb you'll loose definition and clarity in your mix.

The typical mastering processing used on commercial CDs will make the reverbs used in your mix more pronounced. As we discussed in the previous chapter, compression makes the quieter parts louder and the louder parts quieter. Since reverb tails get quieter as they decay, using lots of compression on the mix will make them more audible. If you are getting your mix mastered, it's a good idea to reference your mix with a little "homemade mastering" to hear how the processing affects your wet/dry balance.

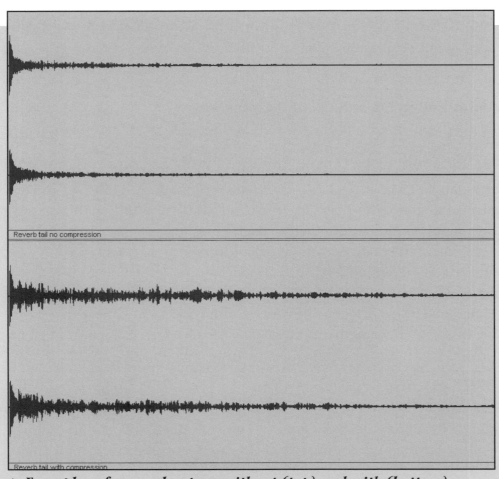

Reverb tail no compression

Reverb tail with compression

▲ *Examples of a reverb return without (top) and with (bottom) compression; in the bottom example, compression has made the reverb more audible.*

Which Instruments Should Have Reverb On Them?

All of them…and none of them…and just some of them! How's that for a vague non-answer? But seriously, most pop mixes use reverb at least on vocals and drums. Certain instruments tend to "like" certain types of reverbs better than others. Plate reverbs, for example, usually work well on vocals and snare drums. Large halls or churches can be nice on choirs and strings. Music style often dictates which elements get doused in reverb. Some aggressive styles of rock can be nearly totally dry, while some pop productions use really big, lush plates and halls on almost every instrument in the mix. Use your judgment, and be careful not to over think it. When you land on something that sounds good, go with it!

Delay

What is Delay, and Why Do I Need It?

Delay…delay…ay…ay…ay…processors record an audio signal then play back repetitions after a user-defined period of time. The delayed signal may be played back multiple times and/or sent back into the original signal, creating a repeating, decaying echo effect. Like reverbs, delays can be used for creating a sense of space in the mix, or for achieving special effects.

Types of Delay Processors

Delay types include analog tape delays, rotating magnetic drums, solid-state analog delay circuits, and digital delays. Most DAWs (digital audio workstations) come with a nice built-in selection of delay processors; some even mimic the old-style tape delay units. But whichever types of delays you have at your disposal will have similar controls.

▲ *Example of a stereo delay*

The Controls

Delay Time/Tempo Sync

This setting controls the delay's repeat rate, and it is usually measured in milliseconds or beats per minute. Since delays are time-based, repeating effects, it's useful to be able to match the timing of the delay to the tempo of the song. If you are working on a DAW, it's easy to synchronize the delay time with the song tempo with the touch of a button. However, if you are using an outboard processor, you'll need to be able to match the timing of the delay with the song. To figure this out, you'll need to be able to convert beats per minute (bpm) into milliseconds (ms). First, find the value for your quarter-note (for our purposes, the basic beat unit of measurement), then divide 60,000 by bpm. If your song tempo is 120 bpm, dividing 60,000 by 120 will give you a value of 500 (60,000/120 = 500). A setting of 500 ms on your delay will result in a quarter-note pulse at 120 bpm. If you want an eighth-note pulse at 120 bpm, just divide 500 ms by 2. If you want sixteenth-note pulses at 120 bpm, divide 500 ms by 4, and so on:

NOTE-TO-BPM CONVERSION

Quarter-note: 60,000/bpm

Eighth-note: (60,000/bpm)/2

Sixteenth-note: (60,000/bpm)/4

Feedback

This sets the number of repeats for the delayed signal. A lower value will have fewer repeats and higher value will have more.

Mix, Wet/Dry, Blend

This control sets the balance between the dry, unprocessed signal and the effected signal.

Delay In Use

If your reverb choices aren't quite working for you, try using a delay! Or, use delays and reverbs together. I almost always use a combination of delays and reverbs to achieve a sense of space and dimension in the mix. Short delay times with a low Feedback setting provide a slap-back sort of effect. Longer delay times with a higher feedback setting create the type of effect that you might typically associate with a big-haired rock guitar solo. Using multiple mono delays, panned hard left and hard right with different delay times, can really widen the stereo image of any source. And vocals and delays go together like chocolate and peanut butter. You can set up a delay using aux sends and returns in same manner as you did with reverb in the previous chapter. Or you can use them as an insert on a specific audio track. I'd say that 80% of the time, I use the aux send approach for delays.

Courtesy Bobby Owsinski

Bruce Swedien *is a Grammy Award-winning audio engineer and music producer best known for his work with Quincy Jones, and having mixed and assisted in producing Michael Jackson's Thriller. He also recorded and mixed for jazz and pop artists such as Count Basie, Duke Ellington, Dizzy Gillespie, Quincy Jones, Herbie Hancock Natalie Cole, Mick Jagger, Paul McCartney, Diana Ross, Barbra Streisand, Donna Summer and Sarah Vaughan. Swedien pioneered the "Acusonic Recording Process" which involves pairing up mics together on vocals and instruments to achieve an enhanced, roomy, ambient sound.*

Let's set up a delay feed into a reverb for a vocal track. The first thing you'll need to do is go to an open stereo auxiliary track. (Or, create one if you're working in a DAW.) Insert a stereo delay on this track. Now, go to the lead vocal track and set up an aux send to feed the aux channel where you just inserted the delay. Raise the aux send to 0 dB and bring up the fader on the delay aux track. For this exercise, we'll go for a slap-back effect on the delay. Set the delay time to something short, like 30 ms. If your stereo delay has separate settings for the left and right channels, set one side about 15 ms later than the other one. Set the Feedback to 4 on the left side and 8 on the right side. Be sure the wet/dry or mix balance is set to 100% full wet. Start playback with the vocal and delay track soloed and listen to the effect. Notice how the left and right side sound with different delay and feedback times.

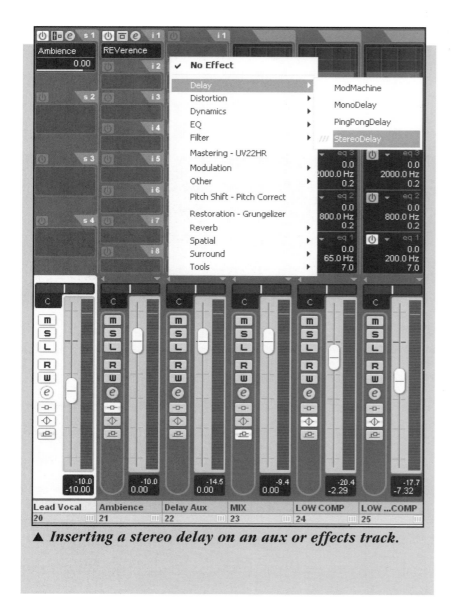

▲ *Inserting a stereo delay on an aux or effects track.*

▲ *Setting up an aux send from the lead vocal into the delay.*

Let's route the delay into a reverb via an aux send. Go to another stereo aux track and insert a plate reverb. Set that to 100% wet with a predelay of about 70 ms. Set the length to about 1.5 seconds. Go to your delay track and using an aux send, send its signal to the reverb track. Set the level on the aux send to 0 dB. Start playback with the vocal, delay and reverb tracks all soloed, and notice how adding the reverb changes the "space" around the vocal. Adjust the fader levels on the delay and the reverb return faders so you are happy with the overall sound. That's all there is to it!

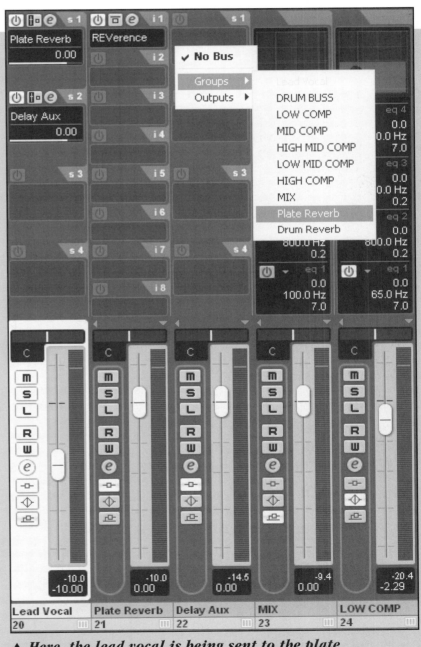

▲ *Here, the lead vocal is being sent to the plate reverb and the delay. The delay signal is also being routed into the plate reverb.*

Another common application for delays is as an insert on individual audio tracks; this setup is especially common for electric guitars. The guidelines for setting up the delay parameters are pretty much the same as they are if you are using the aux send/return approach; the main difference is the way you set the wet/dry balance on the delay. If you are using a delay as an insert on an audio track, you don't want to set the mix parameter to 100% wet. If you did that, you would only hear the delay effect and none of the original signal.

From this point, you can experiment with adding multiple delays and reverbs on different aux channels or even inserting them on the same channel in a serial connection one right after the other. Delay processors are a big part of creating a sense of space, depth, and a wide stereo image in your mix. Use your ears—and by now, you should know that if it sounds good, it is good!

*Through **Al Schmitt**'s career he has been successful as both a recording engineer and record producer. After serving in the U.S. Navy he began working at Apex Recording Studios at the age of 19. In the early 1960s he moved to RCA in Hollywood as a staff engineer where he engineered albums for Henry Mancini, Cal Tjader, Al Hirt, Rosemary Clooney, and Sam Cooke. He also did a lot of motion-picture scoring work for Alex North and Elmer Bernstein. In 1966 Schmitt left RCA and became an independent producer, producing albums for Jefferson Airplane, Eddie Fisher, Glenn Yarborough, Jackson Browne and Neil Young. In the mid '70s he began spending more time engineering again, recording and mixing artists including Willy DeVille and Dr. John among many others.*

CHAPTER 6 OTHER EFFECTS

Modulation Effects

Modulation effects include flangers, choruses, phasers, tremolos, vibratos and rotary-type processors. These processors are similar in that they all create some type of sweeping, swooshing or pulsing effect that can produce a wider stereo image. They can simulate outer-space sounds, Leslie (rotating-horn) speaker cabinets or totally bizarre robot-type effects, or just perform simple doubling. The most widely used modulation effects are choruses, phasers and flangers. These types of modulation effects add a pitch-shifted, delayed version of the signal to the original signal—an effect originally intended to give the sense of multiple instruments playing the same part at the same time. While using chorus, phase and flange effects will create a sense of a bigger and wider sound, they will also cause a less-defined, "washy"-ness within the context of the mix. The phase and pitch shifting can also cause some phase cancellation (instruments disappearing or being drastically reduced in volume) when the mix is summed to mono, so you should be aware of the pitfalls in addition to the pleasures of using these tools.

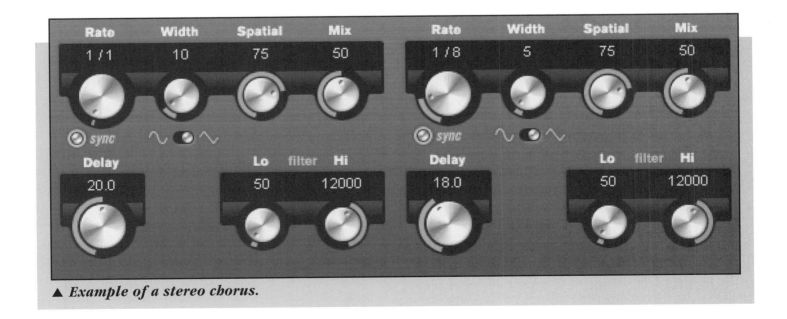

▲ *Example of a stereo chorus.*

Tremolo and vibrato are sometimes used interchangeably, but they are different effects. Tremolo refers to periodic amplitude or volume variation, and vibrato is the periodic variation of pitch or frequency. Pulsing tremolos and vibratos are probably most often used as guitar and electric piano effects. And finally, rotary-type processors create a "swirling-around-the-room" effect like a spinning Leslie speaker cabinet.

Modulation effects go through cycles of being in vogue, and overuse of these effects can easily ruin a mix. But when used in small amounts or in the right context, they can create a nice moment in a mix. Like with all other effects, let your ears and creativity determine how and when they should be used.

Distortion

Sometimes, it is actually desirable to overdrive an audio signal until it begins to break up or saturate. Distortion can add subtle warmth, sustain or thickness to the sound, or it can be used in an over-the-top manner that can often be interpreted as obnoxious or unpleasant. Distortion can do wonders for vocals, guitars, bass, drums, synth pads, organs, or just about anything else—including the entire mix, when used in the right context. There are many types of distortion effects, including valve or tube overdrive, transformer clipping, distortion effect pedals, speaker distortion, and effect-based computer plug-ins. Each type is unique and will result in a different sound; you will need to familiarize yourself with the specific tonal characteristics of each tool at your disposal to effectively use them in your mixes.

▲ *Digital tube overdrive simulator.*

The first time I tried distortion on a lead vocal, I was surprised by the effect. I was mixing a song that was energetic and rocking, and the lead vocal was a bit wimpy in comparison to the music tracks. I was trying everything I could think of to get the vocal sound to match the track. Then I figured I'd try some overdrive, since nothing else was really doing it for me. Much to my surprise, it worked! I used a plug-in that simulated a tube limiter. I loved it in the context of the mix, but when I listened to the track in Solo mode, I hated it! I was really distorting the vocal a lot, but it sounded great in context of the song.

In addition to distorting individual tracks, it can be a wonderful thing to get some saturation going on your entire mix. I have a wonderful-sounding tube EQ that I sometimes patch into my stereo mix bus—but I don't use it for its EQ filters as much as for the tube saturation I get out of it. When I drive the input to the tubes, it just gives this amazingly colorful sound to the entire mix. If I hit it too hard, it starts to sound bad, but using just the right amount of it is magic.

Stereo Image Enhancement

We all could use a little image enhancement at times, don'tcha think? Sometimes our mixes need it, too. Stereo image processors manipulate the stereo image through the use of mid-side (center) processing, which widens and narrows the stereo image by adding and subtracting channel information. While these processors can make a stereo image wider, they can also cause odd phase-y effects if taken too far. These processors should not be used to compensate for an otherwise muddy mix; they should only be used as enhancers, and when adding them to your mix, you should always check the mix in mono to make sure you don't get phase cancellation. In addition to using stereo image enhancers n the overall mix, try them out on various stereo tracks and buses within your mix. Just be careful, and use your ears.

▲ *Stereo image enhancer.*

BEFORE YOU START YOUR MIX

Editing

Since this book is about mixing, I don't want to spend too much time discussing other elements of the production process; but as a mix engineer, you'll probably run into instances where you'll be asked (or expected) to edit the audio material because of timing inconsistencies or other performance problems. My advice is to listen to all of the tracks carefully before you begin mixing, to see if any editing is needed. If you do need to edit, perform this on the front end. Spending too much time and effort in the editing cave can burn you out on a song really quickly. It is so easy to lose inspiration and the important first impression the song makes on you by getting bogged down in the black hole that is editing. So for creativity's sake, either have someone else edit the tracks, or do it yourself before you even think about starting the mix.

Vocal Tuning

It's sad, but true: Not every singer has perfect pitch or perfect control over his voice. Today, it has become expected that the vocals are going to be tuned at some point during the production process. Personally, I have made the decision not to get involved in that process, because to me, it is like fingernails on a chalkboard. So, I do not include vocal tuning as a service I offer. However, I am able to use a few vocal-tuning software programs if necessary. It is also important that you as a mix engineer understand those tools, whether or not you choose to offer tuning services, especially if you are producing and mixing your own material and you have no other options.

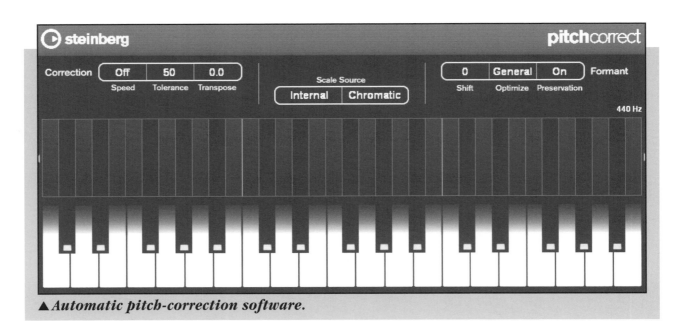

▲ *Automatic pitch-correction software.*

There are two primary uses for using pitch correction. The most obvious is to make out-of-tune sources in tune. This process is not limited to voices; I've had to tune stringed instruments like double bass or cello. Tuning can also be used to quickly fix a note in a guitar solo that doesn't quite fit in the chord. However, like with editing, I highly recommend that all corrective tuning be done before you begin the mix, because the thought process needed to tune vocals is on the opposite end of your brain from the headspace you need to be in when you mix.

The other application for pitch correction is a more creative use of the software sometimes referred to as the "Cher effect," called that because the use of over-the-top vocal tuning as a special effect was first made popular in her hit song "Believe." This special effect is achieved by setting the vocal tuning software to grab notes unnaturally, so they jump from note to note in a mechanical way. If you decide that this effect is what you're after, approach it just as you would any other decision in the mix—if it sounds good, it is good. (I don't think this effect ever sounds good, but I thought I should put in the book anyway. If you like it, more power to you!)

Courtesy Bobby Owsinski

Benny Faccone *is an eight-time Grammy winner mixer-producer who began as an assistant engineer at the legendary A&M studios in the early 1980s. Benny left A&M to start his engineering career in '86 working with Luis Miguel, KC Porter, Ricky Martin, and Anna Gabriel. Today Benny is a sought after mixer/producer with credits that are rich with diverse artists like Boyz II Men, Sting, Reba McEntire, Selina, Nat King Cole, Barbra Streisand, Enrique, Dizzy Gillespie, Stevie Wonder, Nancy Wilson, Los Fabulosos Cadillacs, Manahattan Transfer, Julio Iglasias and Mana.*

Sound Replacement

Sound replacement is just what the name says it is: replacing one sound with another. This does not mean recording a different take with another instrument; sound replacement is just using a sampled sound instead of the original recorded sound. In mixing this technique is most often used on drum tracks. Why would you want to replace the drum sounds that you or some other engineer toiled tirelessly over so they would perfectly fit the song and production? There are a couple of reasons...

Reason #1
The sounds are just not working in the mix.

Sometimes, no matter how much care and effort go into recording the tracks, you are just unable to make them work for the overall sound you are trying to achieve. That is not to imply that the sounds are bad; they just aren't working in the mix. In fact, I've worked on projects where I have had to replace the drum sounds that I recorded. When I got into the mix, I kept saying to myself, "what was I thinking when I recorded these drums?" I had painted myself into a corner, and I had to get myself out. Hello, drum replacement.

A few different software programs allow for relatively easy drum sound replacement. You can either totally replace the original sounds or blend the samples with the original. If the close-miked sounds are not working, then you may find that replacing all of your close-miked tracks with sample will get better results. However, the drums can begin to sound too separated or disconnected if you completely replace all the drums with samples. A good solution for this is to use the original overheads and room mics in conjunction with the samples. Good use of reverbs can also help to give the sample-enhanced drum kit some cohesion.

Reason #2

The sounds are good but parts of the recording are poor.

An example of this problem is the dreaded hi-hat bleed into the snare mic. While there will always be some amount of bleed from the hi-hat into the snare mic, sometimes the bleed is so bad that it makes the close-miked snare unusable. I've had this probem when the hi-hat was physically too close to the snare drum when the drums were recorded, or the drummer had a heavy right hand and hit the hats too hard, or the drums were recorded in a small, untreated room, which can sometimes cause bleed problems. Regardless of how the bleed got there, you can use sound replacement to fix it. In cases like these, I will usually mix a blend of a sampled snare with the original if I can. I will try to pick a sample that closely matches the original snare drum, or even use a sample of the original drum if possible.

Speaking of using samples of the original drums…acquiring your own set of drum samples is a must if you are going to be mixing on a consistent basis. I always make samples of every drum kit I record. This is a great idea if you know you will be recording and mixing the same drum set. That way, the samples and the originals will be the same instrument, and sound very natural when blended or replaced.

Each drum-replacement application handles recording samples a bit differently. But as a general rule, creating clean Wave files of each close-miked drum and the overhead/room mics should get you what you need. Just have the drummer give you a few different hits of each drum and record them all. You can later decide to make a sample that includes bleed from the other mics, or just use the close mics for your samples. Sometimes I'll want a little more room sound on the snare drum, without including all the cymbal sound that room mics always pick up. If I have recorded my own samples of the kit, I can use the samples of the room mics. I'll then layer those with the original snare and blend in as much "clean" room sound as I want. This works like a charm, and sounds very natural because it is the same kit, in the same room, as the original. Experiment with blending multiple samples as well. I have two snare samples that I use often; one of them is really "cracky" sounding, and the other one is very "meaty." Blending the two of them together with the original drum can give me a great big fat snare sound that makes the listener stand up and take notice.

Some Thoughts on Panning

In the Gold Rush of 1849, meant something entirely different than it does in this book. (Look it up.) When mixing, is the placement of audio in the stereo field. There are no rules as to where things should be placed, but there are instances where you should make some educated decisions. A perfect example is mixing a typical multitracked drum kit.

Most drum kits are recorded with a combination of close mics and distant mics. Usually, you'll have an overhead mic configuration where one mic is placed more to the left side of the kit and one is placed more to the right; these mics are usually intended to capture a stereo image of the drum kit, and are often panned hard-left and hard-right. With a right-handed drummer, the hi-hat will be on the left side (from the drummer's perspective) and the ride cymbal and floor tom will be on the right. In this instance, you would not want to pan the close-miked floor tom, which is on the drummers far right, to hard-left when the overhead hat mic is panned hard-left. Make sense? You will also encounter similar stereo image issues in other scenarios where both close and distant mics are used to capture the same source such as orchestras and choirs. Having said that, I recently mixed a string ensemble and intentionally reversed the on the room mics relative to the close-miked instruments. I just liked it better, so I went with it. Use your ears!

Joe Chiccarelli is an American Grammy Award winning engineer and music producer best known for the huge amount of production work he did in the 1980s, 1990s and 2000s. He produced albums by Kajagoogoo, The White Stripes, Stan Ridgway, Oingo Boingo, Ferron, Sandra Bernhard, Spirit of the West, Counting Crows, U2, The Shins, Radiohead, Elton John, the Cult and countless others. He also engineered Frank Zappa's albums Sheik Yerbouti (1979), Joe's Garage Acts I, II & III (1979) and Tinseltown Rebellion (1981).

Talking about the drummer's perspective reminds me of another oft' debated issue. Should the drum kit be panned in the mix as though the listener is sitting behind the drum kit, or as though he were watching the drummer play onstage? In my opinion, there is no right or wrong answer. Some people prefer one way over than the other, and you will hear done both ways on commercial CDs. My advice is, do whichever you prefer. But when I see 16-year olds "air drumming" as they rock out to the latest musical flavor, they are always drumming as though they are sitting behind the kit. So I usually go with the drummer's perspective to make the air drummers of the world happy.

After you have decided on perspective, you'll need to pan the rest of

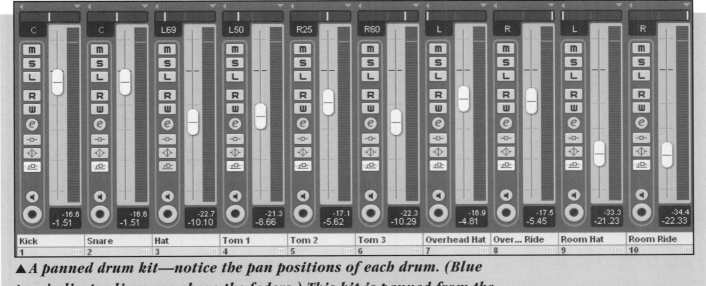

▲ *A panned drum kit—notice the pan positions of each drum. (Blue pan indicator lines are above the faders.) This kit is panned from the drummer's perspective.*

the close-miked drums so they make sense with the overheads. I use one of two approaches. The first is to solo the overheads and pan them hard-left and hard-right. Since the overheads are intended to give you a stereo image of the drum kit, you should be able to hear where in the stereo field the hi-hat and toms occur. All you do then is, pan the close mics to match where drums fall within the overhead stereo image. This is best determined one track at a time. Start with the hi-hat and gradually bring up its fader with the soloed overheads. Move the high-hat in the stereo field so the image doesn't shift at all when you make it louder or quieter. (It should just get louder or quieter.) Now do the same with the toms and any other close mics. The second approach is to disregard trying to get the close mics to exactly match the image of the overheads and just pan everything wherever you want, and let it rock.

Some engineers take a more extreme approach to than others. Some like to really clear out the middle by hard- most of the mix elements, with the exception of the few things they really want to be front and center, like kick, snare and lead vocal. Others take a more thoughtful approach and try not to pile instruments on top of other instruments. really depends on the frequency spectrum of each instrument and other elements occupying the same space in the stereo field. Before you start moving things around, decide what you want to hear and where you want to hear it. Try not to let instruments with the same dominant frequencies occupy the same place in the stereo field.

For instruments that are normally center-panned, such as kick, snare,

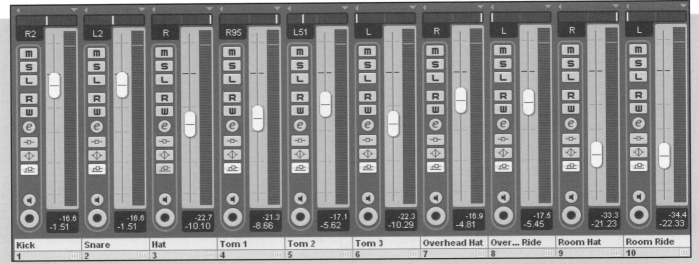

▲*Above, an example of a "harder" approach to drum . Notice that the kick and snare are panned only slightly off-center. This kit is panned from the audience's perspective.*

bass and lead vocals, It can be useful to move these ever so slightly out of the center. Take kick and bass, for example: Try putting the bass guitar just a hair to one side or the other. Try the same with the snare drum. If you like the result, keep it. Remember, the only rule is that there are no rules.

When instruments, don't get into the habit of doing it the same way for every song. Try different ways to widen the stereo image, remembering that minor changes can make a big impact. Making a place for everything in the mix takes lots of practice and experimentation with EQ choices in addition to .

KEEPING IT MANAGEABLE

Getting Organized

I am an odd bird. Certain areas of my life are so disorganized, it's pathetic; but when I start mixing a project, I have to have all my ducks in a row. So I am going to assume that most people are like me and will benefit from an organized approach to mixing. (But if chaos is your muse, go with what works for you...)

For the sake of this example, like others in this book, I am going to assume that you are mixing on a digital audio workstation (DAW)—but the same principles apply whether you are mixing through a console or a DAW. I am also assuming that you are dealing with audio files only—no MIDI or virtual instruments.

It is important to establish an organized and repeatable workflow. The more effort you have to put into physically navigating around your mix, the less energy you'll have to devote to actually mixing the song.

As I said earlier in this book, the first thing I always do is to make sure all editing and vocal tuning has been completed before I start mixing. Nothing kills the energy and mixing vibe faster than having to stop and focus on pitch-correcting a vocal or editing a drum track. To me, mixing is a total shift in focus away from the recording/editing/tuning process and into the realm of creatively, making the most out of the song.

I also believe that a "template" approach to mixing rarely serves the song in the best possible way; I always start with a clean slate. You may know that certain presets or settings work well for certain things, but at the very least, you should listen to the song a few times with all your presets, inserts and settings turned off. For the sake of this example, I'll assume that you'll begin with a blank canvas.

To start, create a blank project and import all of your edited and tuned audio files. If your files have names like "audio 1," "audio 2," and so on, take the time now to rename all the audio files to reflect their actual content. Go through and solo each track to make sure the track name matches the audio material, and change the track and/or file name so everything matches.

Setting Up the Mixer

Now that your files are imported and named correctly, you'll need to lay out your mixer so it makes sense to you. I always start with the drum tracks at the far left, followed by the rest of the rhythm section. I usually put the lead vocals in the center, and the remaining instrument tracks to the right of the vocals. A typical mid-sized track list for a song might look like this:

Kick Inside	Loop R	Organ L
Kick Outside	Tambourine	Organ R
Snare Top	Shaker	Synth 1 L
Snare Bottom	Bass DI	Synth 1 R
Hi-Hat	Bass Amp	Background Vocal 1 L
Tom 1	Acoustic Guitar 1	Background Vocal 1 R
Tom 2	Acoustic Guitar 2	Background Vocal 2 L
Floor Tom	Electric Guitar Rhythm 1	Background Vocal 2 R
Overhead Hat	Electric Guitar Rhythm 2	Background Vocal 3 L
Overhead Ride	Electric Guitar Lead	Background Vocal 3 R
Room Hat	Electric Guitar Color Track	Lead Vocal
Room Ride	Piano L	Lead Vocal Double
Loop L	Piano R	

As you see, I typically have multiple mics for the kick drum, snare drum, toms, overheads and room mics. There are also left and right mics for pianos, keyboards, background vocals and loops. It makes sense to combine these tracks onto group or bus faders so the mix will be easier to manage.

Groups, Buses and FX Returns

For purposes of this example, I am going to talk about group faders and buses as though they are the same thing. Some DAWs have groups and others have buses, but their function is the same in this instance. Combining tracks is a must for manageable mixing. In the above track list, there are 12 drum tracks; that number can easily be cut in half. Here's how: Set up six stereo buses and name them Kick, Snare, Hat, Toms, Overheads and Rooms. Now, route the output of Kick In and Kick Out to the newly created Kick bus. Route the output of the Snare Top and Snare Bottom to the Snare bus. Route the Hi-Hat track to the Hat bus. Route the three Tom tracks to the Toms bus. Do the same for the Overheads and Rooms, and voila—twelve faders down to six!

▲ *An example of drum track routing to buses for more manageable mixing.*
Notice the output routing of all the audio tracks to the new buses.

The track list on the page 82 contains 38 audio tracks. By following the same busing format I just explained, you can shrink the number of faders you need to keep track of during mixing from 38 down to 18. That is so much easier to manage! However, you'll need to listen and decide on a song-by-song basis if busing tracks together makes sense. For example, if Acoustic Guitar 2 is just a double of Acoustic Guitar 1, it would make sense to bus those tracks to one fader. But if Acoustic Guitar 1 is a steel string rhythm part and Acoustic Guitar 2 is a nylon string solo part, it makes more sense to leave them on separate faders.

Once you have grouped or bused your audio tracks, you'll need to move the audio tracks and buses around so the faders you're using in the mix are in a logical order. The whole point of going through this effort on the front end is to let your brain focus on the creative once you start mixing.

Next up are the effects, or FX returns. The FX return fader is used primarily for reverbs and delays—the idea being, if you have eight vocal tracks and you want the same reverb on each track, you can use one reverb instead of eight. For our vocal reverb example, you'll need to create an aux or FX fader in your DAW. Insert a reverb on that track, and name the track "Vocal Verb," or something similar. Next, turn on and route the Aux or FX sends on each of the vocal tracks or buses to "Vocal Verb." Adjust the send level on the individual or group vocal tracks to change the amount of dry signal going into the reverb. You can control the amount of the reverb return (reverb output) in the mix by adjusting the fader level on the "Vocal Verb" FX return track.

You have now taken the dry vocal signal from the tracks and buses and sent that signal to the input of the reverb since it is inserted on the FX track. Multiple signals are being sent into the reverb and the reverb output is now on the fader for easy level control and automation.

For a typical mix starting point, I will set up three or four delays and three or four reverbs. I don't, however, set any parameters on the processors. I just leave them ready for me to start using them when I get to the right point in the mixing process.

Additional Mix Preparations

At this point, editing and tuning should be finished, FX returns and mix elements that can be combined and bused together should be set up, organized, and laid out so they are ready to be mixed. But what if you decide you need more buses or FX returns in the middle of mixing? I usually set up between eight and sixteen spare buses to use during the mix. The only reason I do this on the front end is to avoid having to break the flow while the creative juices are flowing. I may use these buses for parallel compressing, additional FX returns, or to redistribute my original busing scheme. It's just nice to have the extras ready to go in case the song requires them.

It's also good to have the song's time signature, key and tempo information before you start mixing. If you recorded the song, you should already know all this information. If you weren't involved in the recording process, contact the artist and/or producer. If reaching the artist or producer is not an option, you can determine these elements on your own.

Courtesy Bobby Owsinski

Allen Sides *is not only the owner of Ocean Way Recording, he is also one of the most respected engineer/producers in the music industry. As an engineer/producer, Sides' has recorded over 400 albums and won two Grammy's. A brief list of some of the artists he has worked with include: Phil Collins, Green Day, Eric Clapton, Alanis Morrisette, Faith Hill, Trisha Yearwood, Wynonna Judd, Beck, Mary J Blige, Ry Cooder, Joni Mitchell, Frank Sinatra, Ray Charles, Count Basie, Duke Ellington. Ella Fitzgerald, John Williams, Jerry Goldsmith, Tom Newman, Andre' Previn, and Frank Zappa.*

The time signature dictates the number of beats per measure, and figuring it out is as simple as counting the beats in each bar. After you have figured it out, you should set your DAW's time signature to match that of the song. The tempo can be determined a number of different ways. The easiest is to use the beat calculator tap tempo function included in most DAWs. Once the tempo has been determined, you should set the tempo in your DAW to match that of the song. It is a good idea to have a guitar or a keyboard in your mix room so song keys can easily be determined. To do this, just listen to the verses and chorus of the song and play notes on the guitar and/or keyboard until you find the root note or the root chord of the song. Now, set the key in your DAW to the song key, or write it down for later reference.

If working in a DAW, markers or locate points should also be placed at musically relevant places throughout the song. Listen from the top and add markers for each verse, chorus, bridge, solo section and any other applicable location throughout the song.

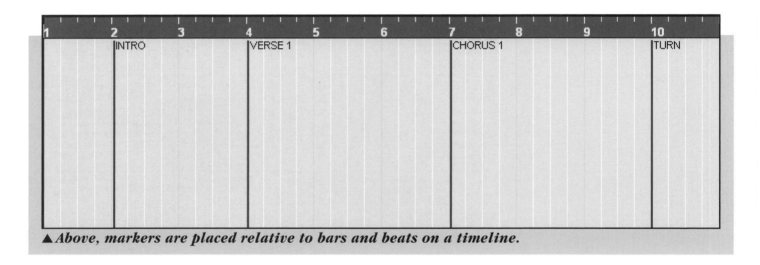

▲ *Above, markers are placed relative to bars and beats on a timeline.*

Now that you're organized and have a handle on the tools, are you are ready to start mixing?

THE MIX!

Deciding On an Approach

Your mix project is now organized and ready to start. But where do you start? It is a great idea to turn every fader all the way down and walk away from the mixing session for a while if you can. For me, it is better for my sanity if I take a short break between the organizational/preparation phase and the start of the mixing phase. But find the method that works best for you within your time constraints.

How do you decide on an approach to take with the song? Start by asking the producer or artist to tell you what they have in mind for the overall vibe and sonic quality of the mix. If they reference other artists, spend a few minutes listening to those artists to get the sound of those mixes in your head. If you are mixing your own material, you should enter the process knowing what you want the final product to sound like. Think it through, and have a clear direction in mind when you begin. You may find that your initial direction and the song's end result are quite a bit different, and that is okay. But if you aim at nothing, then you'll definitely hit it! So start with a plan.

After you have referenced other material, start playback. As the song is playing, bring up the rhythm section and lead vocal faders first, and get a good balance of those elements. Do not turn on any equalizers or compressors or effects yet. Next, add the remaining instruments and vocals, one at a time as the song is playing. You'll probably need to start the song over from the beginning a few times. During this process you need to start deciding where you want to take the mix, what kind of vibe you want to project. As the song is rolling by, determine the elements you want to feature and where they need to be featured. Do you want the drums to be big and roomy, or small and tight? Maybe you want both in different sections of the song? Do you want lots of reverb on the vocals or guitars? What about other special effects? Keep playing the song over and over, as long as you need to, so you have a clear direction for the mix and know which instruments are in each section of the song. You may also find that you have several ideas for possible directions to take the song. When that happens to me, I will spend a little time trying each one out, so I can hear which one works best. Use your imagination. Take notes if you need to, so you can easily recall your first impressions. Go with your instincts and trust your judgment.

During this decision-making process, in addition to getting the mix approach and vibe down, listen for instruments obscuring other instruments in the mix. For example, bringing the piano up to a comfortable level may mask the electric guitars. Or, the organ may get in the way of the vocals. Spend as much time as you need to listen carefully and determine which instruments are "speaking" in which frequency ranges. Notice which instruments are getting in the way of others so you'll have a clear direction when you begin to make EQ choices.

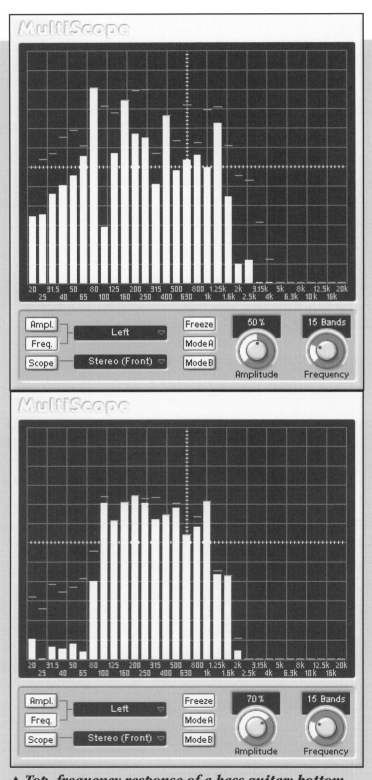

▲ *Top, frequency response of a bass guitar; bottom, frequency response of a string pad. Notice the overlapping frequencies between 100 and 1k Hz.*

Also take note of dynamics: Which parts of the mix have too much dynamic range? Is everything audible throughout the song, or do certain elements appear and disappear many times throughout the song? What is popping out loudly? Decide which elements need to be more up front and which ones need to be farther back. Making these choices now will help you decide which and how much compression, reverb and delay to use.

The whole point to this listening exercise is to have as much of a fully formed plan or target as possible. Try to "hear" the final mix in your head before you begin. Making as many decisions as possible on the front end will enable you to get the mix done more quickly and will usually lead to better results. As you spend more time mixing, you will get quicker at identifying what you need to do to realize your vision for your mix, and your own style will emerge in the process.

Speaking of style, it's a good exercise to try to mimic some of your favorite mixes done by other engineers. This is a really good way to learn what is and isn't effective. Focus on each instrument and try to pinpoint reverbs, EQ and compressors, and see if you can match the process on your mix. I'm not suggesting that you copy someone else's sound, but this technique can go a long way in developing a style all your own when you apply the tricks you've learned from their work with your own creativity.

North and South

I use the term "North and South" to describe listening in mono for competing frequencies and correcting problem areas. (It is much easier to hear frequency build-up and clashes when listening in mono instead of stereo.) I usually start with the low frequencies (South) and work my way to the high frequencies (North). When taking this approach keep in mind that there are many variables to consider when making EQ choices, such as mic placement, instruments used, and the environment in which the source tracks were recorded. You should also know your plan for compressing individual tracks, because compressors can dramatically affect the overall tone of instruments.

Low Frequencies

With your target in mind, switch your speaker control so you are listening to everything in mono, and mute everything except the kick drum. Set the level of the kick drum so it is peaking at about -6 dB on your mix bus. The kick drum usually has a fundamental low frequency between 50 and 80 Hz, depending upon the size and tuning of the drum. To go for a more round kick sound, try adding a peak filter and boosting in that 50 to 80Hz range until the low-end ring of the drum comes through. Adjust the Q setting until you like the way it sounds. Be careful, though; it's easy to go overboard!

Notice the drum's midrange frequencies. If it sounds too honky, insert another peak filter and apply a cut in the 400Hz range. Does the drum need more attack? Add a peak filter and boost in the 3 to 5kHz range. Don't be afraid to experiment with dramatic changes to hear how seemingly wild moves will affect the sound.

Add the bass guitar to the mix. Listen to the way the bass interacts with the kick, and bring its level up so it fits nicely with it. The bass guitar's fundamental frequency is in the same 50 to 80Hz range as the kick drum. You don't want to boost the same frequency in both, because that will lead to a poorly defined bottom end in your mix. If the kick drum was boosted at 60 Hz, try inserting a peak filter on the bass guitar and applying a gain increase at 80 Hz. The point is, you don't want the predominant frequencies of the kick and bass to be occupying the same space.

Add remaining low-frequency instruments, going through the same procedure of carving out space so they can be heard clearly. Be sure that you really want these instruments to be occupying space in this range; for most of my mixes, there is rarely anything else going on in the sub bass range other than bass and kick.

What about the dynamics of the bass and kick? They need to play nice together. Typically, you'll want a good, solid consistent foundation to your low end. While you are making EQ adjustments, add compressors to the kick and bass guitar and go through the exercises you learned in the compression chapter to get them feeling solid. Experiment with the order of EQs and compressors inserted in the signal path to get the best results.

Mid and High-Range Frequencies

Since almost every instrument in most productions occupies at least some of the mid-range frequencies, it can be tricky to make them all fit in the mix without trampling on each other. How should you start sorting this out? Since the lead vocal is the focal point of most songs, it makes sense to make everything else fit around the vocal, so let's start there.

Loop a section of the song where most of the instruments are playing. (Remember, we are still listening in mono to the kick drum and the bass guitar.) Add the lead vocal and make EQ and compression adjustments to make it sound the way you were envisioning in the previous exercise. Listen closely to the way the vocal is interacting with the kick and bass, and make adjustments. For the remainder of this North and South exercise, do not change the level of the vocal; you should be able to get everything else to fit around the vocal just by using EQ and compression.

While still listening in mono, add the rest of the drum kit to the mix. EQ and compress the snare, toms, overheads and room mics to achieve your desired result. Adjust levels so everything is heard clearly. Go through the remaining mid-range and high-frequency instruments, adding them one at a time, while listening in mono. As you are adding each one, go through the same procedure as you did with the kick and bass. Remember what you are aiming for in the mix, and keep that in mind as you are making EQ choices. Don't be afraid to get radical! Try to give each instrument its space, from North to South. After you are satisfied with the way everything sounds in mono, flip your speaker controller back to stereo and begin to pan things around. You will be amazed at how big and clear your mix will sound if you can master the North and South technique.

Build the Foundation First

Another way I approach the mix is to build the foundation first. This method is similar to North and South, but I don't listen exclusively in mono. For this approach, I decide what I want the foundation or feature of the mix to be. By this, I mean I decide which instrument or instruments should really drive the mix, and I start with those. In a rock song, it might be drums and electric guitars. In a pop ballad, it might be piano. It might be a choir in a gospel song. Bring up the foundation instrument and build around it. I will often switch to mono and combine the North and South approach with this method. The only difference is, I put the foundational instruments in the mix first, then add the lows, mids and highs, etc. This helps to keep the feature…the feature! A common variant of this approach is to add the feature instrument after you have the drums and bass in place. Some engineers like to have the rhythm section dialed in before adding anything else.

Start With the Star

This approach is all about the lead vocal. Mute everything except the lead vocal, and get it sounding the way you want it. After you are satisfied with the lead vocal sound and effects, begin adding the rest of the tracks. The order in which you add the rest of the elements is your choice. This method is the same as the foundation example above, except here, you always start with the lead vocal as your foundation instrument. This approach can also be easily combined with the North and South.

All In

As the name implies, this approach is "all in"—all faders are up, and you rarely (or never) solo or mute anything. This forces you to make your mix decisions when listening to the whole, rather than focusing on one instrument at a time. (It's also easy to apply the North and South method while working this way.)

Whether you use one of the methods I described, or come up with your own unique way of approaching a mix, results are what matter most. Just try anything and everything! If it sounds good—and works for you—it is good.

Automation

Repeat after me: "Automation is my friend." Automation is the process of recording and recalling every parameter of every element you choose in your mix. It is a dynamic, not a static, process. This means that if you are recording automation for a lead guitar track and you raise and lower the fader 67 times throughout the solo section, your automation system will "remember" exactly what you did, when you did it, and play it back correctly so you don't have to adjust that fader every time you reach that point in the song. Brilliant!

If you are using a DAW, you can literally automate every possible parameter you can conceive. Some large-format mixing consoles come equipped with extensive automation systems, but are still more limited than a DAW. On most analog consoles, faders and mutes are the only parameters that can be automated with a time reference. That simply means that at any given timecode position, the console will "remember" whether or not the mute is on or off and where the fader is positioned. Digital consoles offer more extensive automation, but a DAW will give you the most control over your mix.

Automation can create motion and movement in a mix; it can add a dynamic element that would otherwise be impossible. It is crucial that you learn the automation system on your chosen mix platform. There are so many benefits to automation that you're really selling yourself short if you don't learn what it is all about.

Simple fader automation is the most basic way to automate a mix. It would be nearly impossible to keep the vocal consistent without some fader rides. Fader automation can also create dynamic movement throughout your mix. One example of this concept is to compress every element in your mix so everything has a smaller dynamic range. This allows the mix engineer to better control the mix by creating dynamic movement with fader automation instead of relying on the performance alone. This method can sometimes give the mix more energy while still keeping the overall dynamics under control. For example, you can easily push drums up in choruses and back down in the verses while still maintaining a consistent feel and sound throughout the song. Your faders should be dancing throughout the song, creating energy and movement from one section to the next. Don't be afraid to push some things far out, while ducking other things. This automation approach gives songs that extra special "something" that the average listener can't quite pinpoint. Try to visualize how you want the song to move, or where and when certain mix elements should be dominant. Experiment, and hear the huge difference fader automation can make.

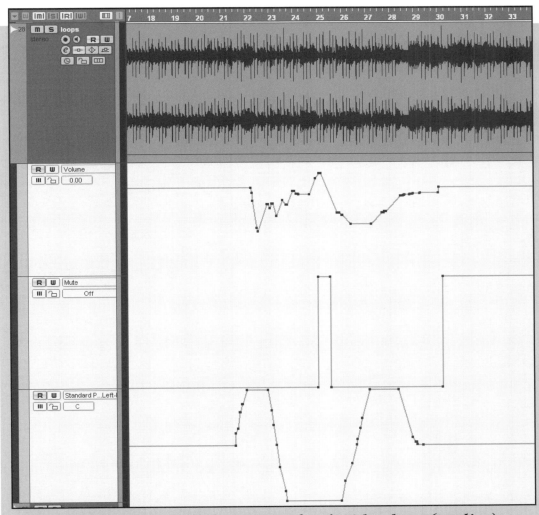

▲ *Above, a stereo loop track (stereo waveform) with volume (top line), mute (middle line) and pan (bottom line) automations. Automation breakpoints can easily be edited to add excitement to the mix.*

It's also common to automate pan settings, EQ settings, compressors, mutes, reverb sends, delay sends, and pretty much anything else you can think of. Let's look at an example of automating a delay send: On the lead vocal track, during a verse the vocal is very dry, with just a touch of reverb and no delay. When the chorus hits, you want the vocal to get big and wide. By automating the delay send from the lead vocal into the delay aux channel, you can adjust the delay so it's audible only in the chorus.

How about automating and EQ? If you have a vocal with a prominent frequency that tends to be a problem in just one phrase in the song, you can set up an EQ filter to notch out the offending frequency—but you don't want the EQ cut happening anywhere but on that one phrase. Automation will take care of this. Just have that EQ band turn on at the appropriate time and turn off after the phrase has passed. Simple and effective.

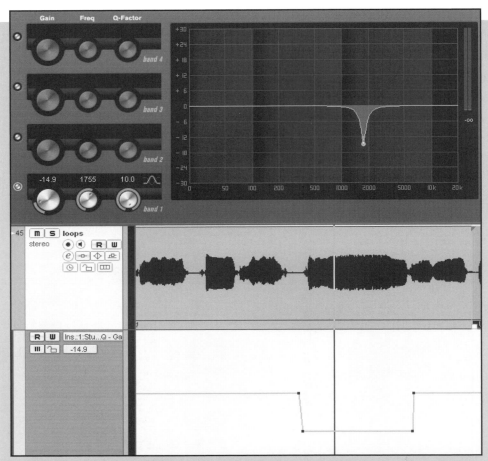

▲ *Automating an EQ to notch out a problem frequency on a single phrase. When the DAW Play head passes over the offending phrase, the gain on the selected frequency is reduced by 14.9 dB but is unaltered before and after EQing.*

Remember the parallel multiband mix compression we set up in Chapter 4? These faders can be automated to bring out certain frequency ranges at certain points in the song. Do you want the choruses to pop a little more? Automate the high-mid compression fader to come up in level, and voila—instant pop!

There are scenarios in which mix compression works well for the verses but not on the bigger choruses. A simple approach would be to automate the Threshold setting on the compressor during the choruses so the mix is being compressed less. Let's say you have a mono percussive synth part that might sound a little boring just sitting in the same spot in the stereo field. Automation to the rescue! Automate the pan setting throughout the song so the mono synth moves from left to right and back again.

Automation is an important step in giving your mix life. And the creative possibilities are only limited by your imagination.

To Sum the Mix...

I once got into an argument with a colleague over a mix I was doing. I was mixing an orchestra, and he told me that the mix was "wrong." I immediately answered, "Wrong? There is no wrong way to mix!"

His point was, he had never heard an orchestra sound the way I made it sound in the mix. That didn't make the mix wrong, it just made it different. I was going for something different than the norm because, let's face it, normal can be boring and mixing music is supposed to be fun and creative. To this day, I'll send that same colleague my mixes, and we'll discuss how "wrong" they are, and we both get a good laugh out of it. But since our initial argument about the "wrong" mix, he has come around to my way of thinking. I hope that you, too, will discover unique and fresh ways to mix music that will inspire your friends to tell you how "wrong" your mixes sound! You never know—your "wrong" way of mixing may be the next "genius" to some. I say all of this to drive home the importance of being unique. Being unique and identifiable is far more important than trying to copy anyone else's style or methods. So, take what you can from this book. If you disagree with my thoughts and ramblings, you can make a few coasters, shims or doorstops out of it. Either way, always remember: If it sounds good, it is good!

INDEX

A

attack 21, 24, 29, 34, 36, 37, 38, 39, 40, 41, 43, 49, 52, 55, 90
automation 3, 84, 92, 93

B

Bus 28, 43. 45, 48, 49, 50, 51, 52, 53
Bus compression 48, 49

C

compression 3, 23, 24, 25, 26, 27, 28, 29, 30, 32, 34, 35, 36, 37, 39, 40, 41, 44, 46, 47, 48, 49, 50, 53, 58, 64, 89, 90, 91, 95

D

de-esser 44, 45, 46
diffusion 59
distortion 22, 24, 32, 39, 72, 73
dynamic range 22, 29, 31, 32, 39, 55, 89, 93
dynamics 27, 29, 30, 32, 37, 41, 48, 49, 54, 89, 90, 93

E

early reflections 59
editing 46, 56, 74, 75, 81, 85
effects returns 60, 83, 84, 85
EQ 3, 7, 8, 10, 13, 14, 15, 16, 18, 19, 20, 21, 32, 33, 37, 41, 43, 44, 45, 46, 49, 51, 52, 58, 59, 63, 73, 80, 88, 89, 90, 91, 94
expander 54, 55, 56

F

feedback 67, 68
frequency 3, 4, 7, 8, 9, 11, 12, 13, 14, 16, 17, 18, 20, 21, 25, 32, 37, 43, 44, 45, 46, 47, 50, 51, 52, 53, 57, 58, 63, 72, 80, 88, 89, 90, 91, 94, 95
FX 83, 84, 85
FX returns see effects returns

G

gain 9, 11, 13, 20, 22, 23, 24, 30, 33, 34, 35, 37, 40, 41, 54, 55, 90, 94

group, groups 28, 45, 47, 48, 49, 51, 82, 83, 84, 83

H

highpass filter 9, 12, 17, 18, 45, 47, 52

K

knee 24, 34, 37, 49, 55

L

limiter 29, 37, 38, 40, 41, 42, 73
lowpass filter 9, 12, 22, 45, 52, 53

M

modulation 71, 72

P

pan (panning) 14, 78, 79, 91, 93, 94, 95
parallel compressor 27, 28, 50, 51, 52
peak filter 9, 18, 19, 20, 90
pitch 8
plate 58, 60, 69
pre-delay 59

R

ratio 23, 24, 37, 54
release 24, 37, 55, 57
reverb 4, 58, 59, 60, 61, 62, 63, 64, 65, 67, 68, 69, 84, 87, 89, 94
rooms 58, 60

S

serial 29, 37, 38, 40, 41, 63, 70
shelving filter 15, 63
sidechain 26
springs 60

T

tempo 35, 57, 66, 85, 86
threshold 22, 23, 24, 25, 30, 34, 37, 39, 41, 43, 54, 55, 56, 57
tuning 57, 74, 75, 81, 85, 90